Productivity Analysis at the Organizational Level

STUDIES IN PRODUCTIVITY ANALYSIS, Volume III

PRODUCTIVITY ANALYSIS AT THE ORGANIZATIONAL LEVEL

EDITED BY

Nabil R. Adam

Ali Dogramaci

Rutgers,
The State University
of New Jersey

Martinus Nijhoff Publishing
Boston/The Hague/London

Distributors for North America:
Martinus Nijhoff Publishing
Kluwer Boston, Inc.
190 Old Derby Street
Hingham, Massachusetts 02043, U.S.A.

Distributors outside North America:
Kluwer Academic Publishers Group
Distribution Centre
P.O. Box 322
3300 AH Dordrecht, The Netherlands

Library of Congress Cataloging in Publication Data

Main entry under title:

Productivity analysis at the organizational level.

(Studies in productivity analysis; v. 3)
Includes bibliographies and indexes.
1. Industrial productivity—Measurement—Addresses, essays, lectures. 2. Civil service—Labor productivity—Measurement—Addresses, essays, lectures. I. Adam, Nabil R. II. Dogramaci, Ali. III. Series.
HD56.P819 331.11'8'072 80-26603

ISBN 0-89838-038-3

Printed in the United States of America

CONTENTS

ACKNOWLEDGMENTS

The editors and the contributing authors are deeply indebted to the referees for their invaluable comments and recommendations and for their numerous suggestions. We would like to express our deep personal appreciation, too, for the thorough and constructive reviewing process provided by the referees whose names follow:

Howard Blum, Rutgers University
Malcolm Burnside, American Telephone and Telegraph Company
Kurt Ingeman, Iona College and Chase Manhattan Bank, N.A.
Nelson M. Fraiman, International Paper Company
Mark Hipp, American Telephone and Telegraph Company
Harvey Hornstein, Teachers College—Columbia University
Holmes Miller, Chase Manhattan Bank, N.A.
I. Douglas Moon, Columbia University
Katherine Morgan, Montclair State College
Frank Sandifer, Georgetown University
Michael Tuschman, Columbia University
Paul Zipkin, Columbia University

1 INTRODUCTION

Nabil R. Adam and Ali Dogramaci

Measuring, analyzing, and improving productivity in a given organization is a complex process that involves the contributions of economists, industrial engineers, operations researchers, management scientists, and lawyers. The objective of this book is to provide the reader with a sample of original papers that relate to these productivity topics at the organizational level. In the book, the word *organization* refers to business firms and municipal organizations.

The book is divided into three parts: perspectives on productivity measurement, a range of studies at the micro level, and some productivity issues in public organizations. Part I, which consists of three chapters, deals with productivity measurement. The first two chapters of this part cover a broad framework of measurement concepts and techniques; the last chapter, on the other hand, provides the reader with an example of productivity measurement for a specific industry (in this case, food retailing). Thus, a spectrum of productivity measurement issues is covered in this part of the book.

While it is almost universally accepted that productivity is a ratio of outputs produced to input resources used, it is also true that there are diverse ways of computing such ratios. Chapter 2 begins with a discussion of these issues. In this chapter, Irving H. Siegel discusses different methods for constructing partial productivity ratio measures (i.e., choices of inputs and outputs to be included as the components of the ratio), as well as alternative methods of measuring a given choice of inputs and outputs. In addition to his survey of various measurement techniques, Siegel presents the main objectives and micro benefits for firms as regards installing and maintaining productivity measurement systems. However, he cautions managers against some of the pitfalls that lead to misusage of such systems. Also presented in this chapter is a brief history of company-based productivity studies that go back to the turn of the century. The literature survey on the topic and the several company examples analyzed by Siegel in Chapter 2 provide guidance and helpful hints to potential practitioners.

Chapter 3 is by John E. Ullmann, who emphasizes the importance of productivity measurement by pointing out that better measurements are essential for improving the efforts to create a higher productivity growth rate. Ullmann's chapter can be regarded as a discussion of some of the limitations of various common measurement approaches. Using illustrative issues drawn from manufacturing industries, he discusses a number of problems in measurement of labor inputs, capital inputs, and outputs. He concludes with a note on value judgments.

Part I ends with a chapter by Hirotaka Takeuchi. This chapter provides a productivity measure developed for food retail chains. The output of organizations within the service industry in general and of a food retailer in particular is viewed as consisting of the tangible products (if any) manufactured in the organization, and the embodied services added to the products at the organization. A method is then developed for determining a man-hour measure of the embodied-service component of the output at a food retailer. To assess the validity of the results obtained from the proposed method, two statistical tests are suggested, and, using the resultant measure of the output, productivity indexes are constructed for labor productivity and total productivity. The input to the labor productivity index represents the aggregate of the working hours of all employees, including managers, administrative clerks, and part-timers. The input to the total factor productivity index is the sum of the man-hour equivalent of labor, capital, and land. Although the methodology developed in this chapter for productivity measurement is outlined within the context of a retail food chain, it can be applicable to businesses or institutions within the service sector that have similar work characteristics.

Part II, in which several studies of productivity at the micro level are presented, begins with a chapter by George Cosmetatos and Samuel Eilon. This chapter develops a set of models to analyze the complex interrelationships between a multitude of variables. The models can serve to answer "what-if" type of questions that typically arise during labor negotiations. Using these models, both labor and management can ascertain explicitly and quantitatively the relative effects of each other's demands on such productivity components as employment, wages, and prices.

The next chapter in Part II is by John C. Panayiotopoulos, who provides an algorithm to solve an operations research problem in the area of human resources and productivity. Specifically, the problem discussed is how to select from among candidates a set of individuals to fill a set of available jobs so that each individual meets a company-defined minimum requirement for the job in which he is placed. The objective is to maximize the total productivity of the individuals over a given period, during which the company's educational, training, and professional development programs are provided to these individuals. The cost of hiring, educating, and training the individuals is not to exceed an allocated budget. A methodology for solving this class of problems is derived, and its efficiency (in terms of computer time and storage requirements) is demonstrated.

After Panayiotopoulos's chapter on an operations research technique for productivity improvement, we move to Chapter 7, by H. JoAnne Freeman and James V. Jucker. This chapter develops the design of an experiment for productivity analysis in an organization. It begins with an extensive literature survey on the topic, with a focus on two types of assembly line organizations—traditional organizations and innovative ones. A set of hypotheses about the performance of traditional versus innovative assembly organizations is presented, which in turn leads to the questions of what measures to use and how to go about testing them. Measures (e.g., turnover, absenteeism, accident rate, and job satisfaction) required to test the hypotheses are then identified, and sources for obtaining such measures are pointed out. To determine if one assembly organization is more productive than the other, several productivity indexes are discussed in terms of purpose, data availability, and measurement issues.

The last two chapters of Part II deal with issues related to industrial economics and address questions regarding whether larger firms or establishments tend to have higher labor productivities. The topic is important in terms of its implications for tax incentives and antitrust policies of governmental agencies. The two chapters serve to highlight the issues raised from opposite perspectives. Chapter 8, by Ellen Susanna Cahn and Lloyd J. Dumas, concludes that industries with higher concentration ratios (i.e., industries in which a larger percentage of the shipments are accounted for by a few establishments) do not tend to generate significantly higher rates of technological progress and productivity. As a policy implication, Cahn and

Dumas tend to favor stronger antitrust policies. On the other hand, the research presented in the next chapter, by Edward M. Miller, reaches a counterconclusion, and, regarding the question of antitrust policies, states that such measures may discourage productivity growth.

These differences are not unusual. Indeed, the literature survey of Cahn and Dumas at the beginning of Chapter 8 points out just that—namely, that for decades researchers have argued counterviewpoints on this matter.

One of the difficulties in reaching a common conclusion is the nature of data available for such studies. This issue is raised by Cahn and Dumas when they describe the imperfections in their statistical analyses that arise from measurement problems. A number of statistical problems are also raised and discussed by Miller. Since we are fortunate enough to be able to present a sample of counterempirical studies, we hope to give readers a choice in reaching their own conclusions about policies, as well as about directions for future research.

The last part of this book, which is devoted to productivity issues in public organizations, begins with a chapter by Emanuel S. Savas. This chapter opens with a discussion of the factors that account for the low productivity of governmental organizations. Such factors include unclear definition of the various government programs, difficulty of measuring a government program's achievement with respect to its goal, and lack of an effective link between the performance of a civil worker and his rewards. It is pointed out that employing alternative public services delivery mechanisms for the same service results in competition, which in turn results in higher government productivity. Although competition leads to increased productivity of governmental organizations, it is concluded that opposition of employee organizations is considered a major obstacle in achieving this competition.

Chapter 11 is concerned with public sector productivity and collective bargaining and is written by a well-known labor arbitrator, Eric J. Schmertz. This chapter provides an analysis of some of the difficulties in implementing productivity improvement programs in the public sector, which is a labor-intensive industry. The issues are presented within the framework of a case study. The focus of the case is New York City, where fiscal and productivity problems have been acute for some time. At the outset of the chapter, the reader is reminded that to improve productivity—no matter how ingenious a work arrangement or mechanization technique may have been developed by a manager or an engineer—the value of such a new technique will be limited so long as unions refuse to accept the implementation. This basic fact highlights the importance of collective bargaining for productivity improvement programs. In the chapter, the important parameters of the problem and recent trends (fiscal difficulties of municipal governments and the impact of inflation on the pressures for cost-of-living adjustments) are analyzed, and the relationships between the various pressure factors are illustrated with examples.

I PERSPECTIVES ON PRODUCTIVITY MEASUREMENT

2 PRODUCTIVITY MEASUREMENT AT THE FIRM LEVEL: *A Brief Survey*

Irving H. Siegel

2.1. DEFINITIONS AND PROXIES

Like the lay public and the media, the business community tends to use the term *productivity* loosely. Nevertheless, many firms do—as many more should and will—show an interest in tracking their own performance in accord with the familiar professional definition. This definition is broad. It admits a wide variety of measures even though it excludes many concepts that also are germane to the monitoring and analysis of company achievement.

In strict professional parlance and practice, *productivity* signifies a "family of ratios of output quantity to input quantity." The words *family* and *quantity* are obligatory despite a frequent failure to include them explicitly in descriptive statements in the technical literature.

So defined, the productivity family is large and is even growing. Thus, many ratios are eligible in the first instance, and many variants are added, in effect, as technical ingenuity is invoked to compensate for deficiencies in the data supply. In the first instance, output, the productivity numerator, may be measured (1) "gross" or "net" in more than one acceptable sense; (2) in terms of end products (the typical case) or component "subproducts''; and (3) either directly (by the ''weighting'' of ''physical'' quantities of individual products) or indirectly (by the ''deflation'' of value by price). The usual productivity denominator refers to labor input, but (1) this input is measurable in more than one way (e.g., with respect to number of employees or their hours, and with or without weights that distinguish ''quality''); (2) other inputs are admissible and of coordinate interest (capital—both fixed and circulating—and intermediate inputs, such as energy and materials); and (3) composites of labor and these other inputs are pertinent also. Too frequently, the productivity indicators based on such composites are grandly miscalled measures of ''total factor'' or ''total'' productivity, but these characterizations will be avoided in this paper.

The term *quantity* deserves additional comment. By courtesy and convention, it is generously interpreted. Thus, it is understood to include weighted aggregates of ''physical'' quantities—aggregates that correspond, say, to price-stabilized dollars or productivity-stabilized man-hours. When indirect methods of estimating such aggregates are used, the results are often fuzzy or casually misinterpreted. In particular, the stabilized dollars are commonly described as ''constant,'' but they may be fixed only with respect to two aggregates entering into one index ratio (as in the Paasche formula) rather than with respect to all the aggregates comprising a set or a series (as in a Laspeyres index covering a number of years). This remark provides a bridge to the next two paragraphs.

Deflation is a deceptively easy technique of indirect estimation used when output or input aggregates (or indexes) cannot be conveniently or at all computed directly from physical quantities. It seems to yield adequate results at low cost in information and time; yet it could mislead if the value dividend and the price deflator do not match closely in *content*. Furthermore, the *structure* of the divisor determines the structure of the quotient, and this fact, too, is indispensable to the correct interpretation and use of the derived numbers.

To show concern for structure as well as content is to show respect for *literal* as well as *verbal* algebra. According to verbal algebra, which operates on dimensions only and involves nothing deeper than a cancellation of words, the quotient of a value index and a price index does represent quantity. A question remains, however: Quantity of just what? The answer is provided, in part, by the actual content of the two measures. The rest of the answer is that the sense of the quotient depends, in addition, on the literal algebra of the case—on the details of construction of the deflator. Thus, even if the dividend and divisor are compatible in scope and content, the explicit formula and weights of the deflator determine the implicit formula and weights of the quotient. The lesson is clear, though too seldom stated and insufficiently heeded: If proper caution cannot be practicably observed in the making of an index number, the burden of vigilance is transferred to an often unalerted user. In short, the true properties of a measure have to be appreciated for proper application and analysis.

2.1.1. A Variant Productivity Definition

At this point, mention should be made of a dual definition of productivity that ought to appeal to companies as a "natural" extension of conventional accounting. Instead of focusing on quantities, we may view productivity as a ratio of prices. Indeed, verbal algebra readily shows that the productivity ratio cited above is equivalent to a *family of ratios of input price to output price.* Moreover, the price and quantity forms can be rendered equivalent according to the stricter requirements of literal algebra—by a judicious selection of index-number formulas and weights. Thus, it is possible to design productivity indexes that satisfy *both* definitions at the same time and that are interconvertible. Although implementation of the price form would appear to be a congenial sequel to normal accounting practice, it has not yet found favor with companies monitoring their own productivity.

It is easy to see, from verbal algebra, the emergence of the price form of productivity. Setting the value of output equal to the value of input, we write $V = PQ = P'Q'$, where V is value, P and Q are the price and quantity of output, and P' and Q' are the price and quantity of input. By merely rearranging terms, we find Q/Q', the quantity form of productivity, corresponding to a price form, P'/P. The most famous case of this verbal or dimensional identity occurs when the value measure for output and input is confined to payrolls, so that Q/Q' refers to output per unit of labor input (say, per man-hour) and P'/P is the ratio of average (hourly) earnings to unit labor cost. As has already been stated, it is possible to make $Q/Q' \equiv P'/P$ a literal algebraic identity as well as a verbal or dimensional one.

2.1.2. Useful Kindred Ratios

Many input-output (or output-input) ratios that resemble productivity but that do not strictly satisfy the quantity definition are encountered in applied economics and econometrics, operations research, systems analysis, industrial and chemical engineering, management science, and other disciplines. These ratios could be put to good service, of course, by companies that seek to improve performance, but their nature should be understood. Neglect of the actual content and structure of such ratios could lead to erroneous application or interpretation. The next three paragraphs elaborate.

The very adjective *input-output* conjures up the coefficients of the Leontief system, cost-benefit ratios, return on investment, and so forth, but we wish to confine attention here to two particular productivity proxies. These ratios suffer from different degrees of price "vitiation"; yet they too can be and have been used to advantage in company improvement programs. One of these ratios refers to value added per man-hour; the other relates value of sales (preferably adjusted for inventory change) to total employment cost (payroll plus fringes).

The first of these two measures has a numerator in which price (more specifically, unit value added) has not been stabilized. Nonetheless, it is often used for comparison of one firm against another, of one establishment against another in a multi-establishment company, or of a firm against its "competition" (the whole industry in which it is located). The last of these comparisons is facilitated by the publication of statistical series on value added per man-hour for hundreds of manufacturing industries by the Bureau of the Census. These figures and the corresponding computations of individual companies could provide more reliable comparisons if the numerators were free of price "noise."

A change in the second proxy from one period to another does not reflect "pure" change in the ratio of output quantity to input quantity unless the price element in both numerator and denominator is fixed. Despite the obvious risk of distortion implicit in neglect of unstabilized price changes, the ratio of sales value to employment cost (actually, the reciprocal) is apparently being used amicably as a "productivity" indicator for bonus-pool estimation in companies that operate under the Scanlon Plan. It would clearly be a mistake, therefore, to assume that only high-grade productivity measures can help companies to improve performance; but it would also be a mistake not to be on guard against statistical surprise and its practical consequences.

Many operating or financial ratios other than value added per man-hour and the share of wages in product value are also published for manufacturing industries by the Bureau of the Census. Accordingly, a wide range of comparisons may be made by companies with the industries in which they are located. Although the ratios are not productivity measures in the strict sense of this paper, they are conceivably useful for helping companies to improve their performance. Again, caution is necessary in interpretation.

2.2. HISTORY AND USE

How extensively and how comprehensively firms practice productivity measurement are not known, but recent circumstances must have encouraged a step-up of formal monitoring activity. The existence of formal programs is not advertised as a rule, perhaps because of the traditional adversary relationship of labor and management in pay determination. Furthermore, as already noted, *productivity* is not always used as a term of art in the business world, and so publicized instances do not necessarily refer to continuing measurement systems that feature the construction of numerous quantity ratios for work centers or departments or of aggregate ratios for divisions or the whole firm; the appraisal and projection of temporal change from such computations; and, perhaps, the use of such computations for interplant or interfirm comparison also.

2.2.1. Recent Incentives to Measure

A dominant circumstance stimulating greater company interest in tracking productivity during the past decade or so has been the unprecedented experience of persistent and vigorous inflation. This inflation began in the mid-1960s with the failure to tax-finance the Vietnam escalation, and it has been subsequently reinforced and extended by the energy-price revolution and by turmoil in the Middle East. It has been supported by, and has in turn supported, wage demands that consistently and sizably outrun labor productivity gains. These gains have slowed perceptibly, and the sluggish (even negative) rates recorded are themselves reflections, in part, of the inhibiting effect of inflation on capital investment. In a world wracked by inflation, U.S. companies have become increasingly concerned with the threats to their profitability, survival, and autonomy that are posed by rising costs and intensifying foreign competition. Counteraction of these threats would be facilitated by the availability of instruments for measuring productivity levels and changes. In present circumstances, such instruments are pertinent for monitoring the use of costly inputs in addition to labor and capital—for example, critical materials and fuels (such as coal and natural gas in the case of electrical utilities).

Less momentous and less pervasive influences have also contributed in recent years to the interest of firms in their own productivity records. One pertinent development of the 1970s was the inauguration of a measurement program covering about two-thirds of the workers in federal agencies. Responsibility for this program is vested in the Bureau of Labor Statistics.

Since government agencies are like companies and since they perform many services that have private counterparts, their experience and example surely exert a positive influence on company resolve and practice. Another significant factor was the revelation in 1972 that firms generally lacked the productivity information required for estimating allowable price increases under the federal economic stabilization program then in force. Still more recently, in 1975, the Department of Commerce began holding seminars for businessmen on the merit and methods of company productivity measurement; and, in 1976, the now defunct National Center for Productivity and Quality of Working Life conducted a conference that echoed the Commerce theme of company productivity improvement through company productivity measurement.

2.2.2. Roots of Company Monitoring

World War II and its aftermath of growth and reconstruction provided fertile ground for the spread, if not the actual start, of formal productivity measurement at the level of the firm. During the war itself, defense plants, especially those engaged in airplane assembly and shipbuilding, were challenged to meet urgent and ambitious production schedules in a regime of manpower stringency. Shortly after the war, the Bureau of Labor Statistics was able to initiate and successfully conduct a multi-industry program whereby companies directly reported changes in the unit man-hour requirements of their chief products. This program, which lasted into the early 1950s, familiarized participating and nonparticipating companies with the techniques and benefits of measurement. It supplied labor weights for use in both industry and company productivity tracking. It was imitated in a few other U.S. studies undertaken to assist European economic recovery in the spirit of the Marshall Plan. Perhaps more important was its contribution of information, expertise, and insights for interfirm and interplant comparisons and analyses made by European students.

Looking backward to the 1930s, we find that the potential for company measurement was strengthened by federal action to improve the national data base, which included the conduct of field studies. The Bureau of the Census, already compiling industry statistics on the basis of a biennial canvass of manufacturing establishments, began publication of industry summaries on value added per man-hour. The Bureau of Labor Statistics began systematic collection of establishment reports on employment and hours and made field investigations of productivity performance in selected industries. A special contribution to productivity measurement on the industry and company levels was made by the WPA National Research Project on Reemployment Opportunities and Recent Changes in Industrial Techniques, which flourished in the half decade preceding World War II.

Still earlier adumbrations deserve mention. One is scientific management, which came onto the industrial scene before World War I. The war provided a crucible for testing and refining the principles and procedures of scientific management, which included "work measurement" (in labor time and money) and "cost accounting." Notice must also be taken of the pioneering investigations of C. D. Wright, the first commissioner of labor, into company productivity and costs. His massive report of 1898, entitled *Hand and Machine Labor,* remains an awesome landmark.

2.2.3. Applications of Company Figures

A company that installs a measurement system has a source of current statistics usable for many informational, analytical, and decisional needs. The potentials offered by the emerging figures are not, of course, automatically realizable. A measurement system's efficacy depends, in part, on the appropriateness of the system's design to the company's perceived requirements. A system should also be introduced and administered with due regard to the quality of labor-management relations, and it should be coordinated with other extant managerial programs. Like any other intended tool of management, productivity monitoring can degrade to a toy if it is used apathetically or trivially and if it is not maintained in realistic accord with changing company structure and markets. Still worse, a management tool that is misused can turn into a dangerous weapon.

When a company decides to embark upon monitoring, it can acquire an early benefit by adroit dissemination of the news. The very announcement can promote consciousness of the need to upgrade performance and of the opportunities for doing so. This favorable announcement effect may be reinforced by timely and voluntary assurance that the numbers will be used fairly and that the system will be progressively revised with growth of experience and sophistication in its use.

A company that starts with either an end-product or subproduct bias will soon discover that both orientations have their merits. End-product measurement, suggested by practice at and above the industry level, is particularly suited to the outward-looking purposes of the headquarters staff and the higher echelons of management—for example, planning, forecasting, and comparisons of performance. A subproduct emphasis, which may suggest itself where work measurement has been tried, is well adapted to control of operations and costs; it could lead to early and significant payoffs even if confined to critical departments or activities.

In the scattered literature on company measurement of productivity, applications like the following are mentioned as feasible or actual:

Anticipation, diagnosis, and timely correction of operational dysfunctions;
Appraisal, by means of before-and-after productivity comparisons, of the efficacy of intended remedial actions;
Provision of recurrent agendas for labor-management dialogue, which could eventually extend beyond measured productivity performance to other matters of mutual concern;
Adjustment of operational workloads and worker assignments;
Establishment of realistic hiring and training schedules;
Improvement of work routine and plant layout;
Timing of equipment and process changes;
Revision of make-or-buy patterns;
Cost control by means of targets for reject reduction and for unit requirements of labor, capital, energy, and materials;
Pay and bonus administration;
Budgeting;
Indoctrination of junior officials, managers, and line supervisors.

2.3. NUMERATORS AND DENOMINATORS

2.3.1. Output Varieties

A company that opts for end-product measurement may be satisfied at first with figures for sales, shipments, deliveries, or completions. However, it will soon find reason for introduction of a more representative indicator of output. In particular, it may decide to get closer to "gross output" or "production" by the adjustment of sales or shipments for change in inventories of finished and unfinished goods.

The adjusted sales or shipments are "gross" in several senses. Like the unadjusted figures, they still overstate the economic contribution of the company's labor and capital inputs; they remain swelled by the value of energy, materials, and so forth, purchased from other firms. Furthermore, they may be "gross" from the standpoints of industry-wide and economy-wide summation; that is, they have not been purged of the output fractions destined for "consumption" (as materials, etc., but not as capital) during the same period by other firms located in the same industry or other industries. For company productivity tracking, however, this kind of grossness needs no purging. A consolidated company measure should, on the other hand, avoid the double counting of interplant transfers.

Rarely is it practicable, although it would be desirable, to measure a firm's entire output by the weighting of physical quantities of individual products. Ideally, the weighted aggregates based on incomplete physical data should be rounded upward for exhaustiveness; price assumptions are sometimes invoked for this purpose, but the need for adjustment is commonly ignored. Another problem that is often left unresolved is the adjustment of quantities of individual products to refer to constant-quality equivalents through time. The indirect method of output estimation by means of price-deflation of values, to which companies make generous resort, may appear to avoid or to overcome the challenges of direct measurement, but the results are not necessarily reliable. As noted earlier, deflation transfers burdens from indexmakers to indexusers.

A company may wish to "nettify" its measure of gross output as a first, or sufficient, venture into the monitoring of net productivity. Here, the weights applied to the individual products represent less than full unit price. Thus, they could refer to unit value added, unit labor cost, or unit manhour requirements. At least in principle, the same output measure is obtainable indirectly—by the deflation of an appropriate dividend by an appropriate divisor.

The classical Census concept of value added offers another net-output model that a company, a more ambitious one, may wish to implement. Value added equals the difference between the value of gross output and the value of utilized energy, materials, and so forth that are purchased from other firms. To represent "quantity," the minuend and subtrahend have to be expressed as aggregates with stabilized prices. The stabilization is often attempted by the introduction of separate deflators—the method of "double deflation." The constant-price aggregates so derived, however, are sometimes eccentric—even negative. This contingency, which cannot be ruled out in a period of serious inflation, confers a greater respectability than would otherwise be warranted on the simpler "nettified" measure mentioned in the preceding paragraph.

Two other net concepts are suggested by the Census notion of value added. Both are netter and are encountered in national income and product accounting. One of these variant concepts is an analogue of "gross national product": The subtrahend includes not only consumed energy, materials, and so forth obtained from other firms but also purchased services, such as telephone, computing, and advertising. The second variant, which corresponds to "net national product," has a still larger subtrahend that includes allowance for capital consumption.

From the preceding remarks, it is clear that a company could try to tailor a net-output concept to match exactly the scope of the input denominator of a productivity ratio. Thus, output and input may be viewed as two faces of the "same" set of resources. Indexes of productivity derived from such output and input measures have attractive properties from the standpoint of literal algebra. Suffice it here to say that these particular productivity indicators are not at all constrained by their nature to show no change through time.

The gross and net concepts thus far considered feature end products, but a company could just as well look upon its activity—instead or in addition—in terms of subproducts. This alternative approach is relatively uncommon, but it has intuitive appeal and offers many advantages.

Subproducts are the components that make up salable or shippable end products. In the case of services, they are the necessary intermediate accomplishments that underlie the deliverable results. They are the contributions of strategic work centers or cost centers; or they may be associated with the activities of sequences or clusters of centers. Preferably, they should be measured as physical quantities, which could be weighted (e.g., by direct money or man-hour cost per unit) for the derivation of weighted aggregates. The aggregation of subproducts is achievable, just as in the case of end products, without duplication and without confusion between output and input. Where work measurement is already practiced, a data base for some of the required information may already exist.

Measurement on a subproduct basis permits development of productivity indicators that are more sensitive to the patterns of economic activity actually pursued within companies. Accordingly, it is well suited to the interest of managerial control—to the fine-grain scrutiny of company operations. It allows direct approximation of change in inventories of finished goods and work in process. It is applicable to situations in which end products are complex assemblies or the results of progressive processing of a key material, show extreme heterogeneity, have long production cycles, or include variable mixes of parts made in-house or purchased from outside.

2.3.2. Input Varieties

A company that sets up a productivity-tracking system normally starts with a labor denominator, but it often proceeds no further. Many reasons may be cited for the common confinement of the denominator to output per employee (total, so-called production workers only, etc.) or to output per man-hour (compensated, spent at the work place, actually worked, etc.), weighted or unweighted with regard to pay. It is realistic for a company to begin modestly and to go forward incrementally. After some experience, it may find that a labor-productivity system is adequate to its needs, especially when used in conjunction with accounting information and other extant data sources. Among the other plausible deterrents to the extension of the battery of productivity measures are inertia, limitations on the supply of required data and in-house quantitative skills, flagging or uncertain top-level commitment or support, lack of managerial sophistication, and expectation that additional benefit would not warrant additional cost.

The logical next step in the extension of productivity measurement would seem to be the coverage of capital input, but this step is not an easy one and could be deferred with impunity. Indeed, a company may be well advised to skip over capital to a critical intermediate input that is in short supply, like energy or a material. Meanwhile, an approach to capital measurement might be developed by relevant company staff on the basis of a survey of the voluminous literature on the subject, including a review of measures actually used by other companies (see Section 2.4.2) and an inquiry into the state of company information on capital acquisitions, retirements, depreciation, asset lives, expenditures, and so forth.

The "quantity" of capital input is not so intuitively obvious a notion as the "quantity" of labor input. In view of the controversy still heard in scholarly circles, no claim can plausibly be made that a particular mode of measurement is definitive. Furthermore, many of the measures actually made are of doubtful quality and cogency, despite their evidences of patient and ingenious ministrations to available data. A company ought not to be encouraged to add a low-grade measure of capital productivity to its system simply out of mimicry or for the appearance of completeness.

Capital includes many varieties, and each poses its own challenges of reduction to a constant-dollar magnitude. The category that is of greatest interest for productivity measurement is, of course, fixed capital, which comprises many elements (plant, equipment, and, as a rule, land also) purchased at different times and having different expected useful lives. The capital denominator commonly includes inventories in addition; and some company measures even take cognizance of accounts receivable, cash, notes, and so forth.

The more careful estimates of "real" capital services are derived by labyrinthine procedures (e.g., the perpetual-inventory method) that require assumption and judgment all along the way. Some students prefer a "gross" concept of fixed capital stock (unadjusted for depreciation) to "net"; and some would take account of variation in the rate of capacity utilization. Differences of opinion and practice are also manifested with regard to asset lives, depreciation schedules, relevant interest rates, conversion of acquisition prices to base-period prices, computation of net rental weights, the treatment of force-account construction, the inclusion of leased equipment, and so forth.

In time, the availability of company information for estimating capital input should improve somewhat as a result of action taken in September 1979 by the Financial Accounting Standards Board. The board's statement no. 33 calls for a start toward "inflation accounting" in company reports for fiscal year 1980. Current-cost figures are requested for depreciation, depletion, and amortization, as well as for net assets (inventories, plant, equipment, and "property").

A company that wants to go beyond labor-productivity monitoring need not fear handicap through failure to follow two authoritative fashions of the national scene. One of these is to try to separate advance of "knowledge" from the capital containing it. The other is to regard a hard-won measure of composite labor-capital productivity as just a "measure of ignorance," a "residual" that requires further resolution into contributions of additional variables. This is not a proper forum for critical appraisal of these fashions. A point already made can bear one more repetition: Whatever kind of measure a company devises is constructively usable if it is interpreted with serious regard to its explicit content and structure.

The same point is applicable to measures relating to intermediate input, especially measures obtained by means of deflation. Another point of some interest to companies that attempt to compute indexes of productivity with net-output numerators should be mentioned here: The subtrahends of the value-added numerators (i.e., energy, materials, etc. expressed in stabilized prices) are usable as denominators also for company measures of productivity featuring *gross* output.

A concluding observation is directed particularly to companies that proceed to the measurement of energy productivity before attempting to quantify capital stock. From the standpoint of productivity estimation, capital *stock* is simply an intermediary for the determination of periodized capital *services*. It should be considered, however, that changes in energy input (preferably differentiated into components for the lighting and heating of plant and structures and for the operation of equipment) may satisfactorily and economically reflect changes in the services rendered by capital stock. Experimentation in the use of energy input as a proxy for capital services is accordingly recommended.

2.4. COMPANY EXAMPLES

Considerable guidance for company measurement of productivity is available in the meager, dispersed literature. In addition to manuals, like those by Greenberg (1973) and by Kendrick and Creamer (1965), there are many articles describing the systems tried in various companies.

The literature also treats the two kinds of proxy labor-productivity indicators mentioned earlier in this paper. Thus, value added per man-hour has been used in interestablishment comparisons for U.S. manufacturing industries by Klotz, Madoo, and Hansen (1980); and value added per man-hour or per employee has been used in European studies by Pratten (1976*a*, 1976*b*). The reliance of Scanlon Plan companies on the second kind of proxy, which relates current-dollar sales (or production) to current-dollar labor expense, is illustrated in a monograph by Moore (1975).

Finally, helpful hints for the design, development, and conduct of company (and government-agency) systems of productivity monitoring are offered in many places. Relevant information is contained, for example, in reports of the Joint Financial Management Improvement Program (1977), National Center for Productivity and Quality of Working Life (1975), U.S. Civil Service Commission et al. (1972), and U.S. Department of Energy (1978*a*, 1978*b*). Also pertinent are writings by Bernolak (1976), Carr (1973), Kraus (1978), and Siegel (1976, 1980*a*, 1980*b*); and Chapter 8 of a report prepared by the Panel to Review Productivity Statistics for the National Academy of Sciences (1979).

2.4.1. Labor-Productivity Examples

The practical Kendrick-Creamer handbook (1965) gives six examples of company productivity measurement, two of them referring to labor input. The two companies are cited by name, General Oil and International Business Machines Corporation.

The output numerator for General Oil is based on aggregates of physical quantities—refinery products (ten classes); natural gas and petrochemicals, each weighted by unit value; and imported residual fuel oil, weighted by unit value added. The labor denominator refers to unweighted hours—paid, rather than actually worked—of all employees. It excludes the hours of construction workers and laboratory employees, whose output is not represented in the numerator.

The output index of International Business Machines Corporation approximates real value added. It was computed by deflation of net intramural production cost (i.e., direct labor plus overhead) of parts, subassemblies, and final assemblies by a closely matching measure of in-house unit cost. Double counting was avoided in this indirect subproduct approach, and no adjustment was required for inventory change. Labor input was computed in terms of full-time employee equivalents—separately for direct and indirect workers and for all combined. Separate productivity and cost measures for the company's various plants permitted useful comparisons of performance. The cost series also proved valuable for make-or-buy decisions. The present author served as consultant in the decision of the IBM measurement system.

Another case, studied by Sherrard (1967) as a doctoral candidate, refers to labor productivity in the multi-unit St. Paul and Tacoma Lumber Company in selected years of the interval 1903–1938. Lumber output was measured in board feet; and other products, like lath and shingles, were converted to board-feet equivalents. The employment denominator included hours of all personnel, except for top management, engaged in lumber operations; it omitted workers in logging camps or transporting logs to sawmills. Separate productivity measures were computed for different activities and sites—in addition to the measure for the whole company.

A fourth labor-productivity example concerns the Mill Products Division of the Aluminum Company of America. This productivity measure, reported by a high company official, Gantz (1976), goes back to 1968. It was patterned, for maximum comparability, on the Bureau of Labor Statistics index of output per man-hour for the aluminum-rolling-and-drawing industry as a whole.

A fifth illustration, due to Peck (1976), is the use of a battery of labor-productivity ratios for monitoring the performance of wholesale-grocery warehouses. These ratios, expressed in tons per man-hour, relate to such activities as car unloading (unitized), car unloading (manual), backhaul unloading, order selection, truck loading, and truck repacking, as well as to all "department" activities combined.

Our final example for labor productivity concerns a company's use of "work measurement," which economic statisticians often take pains to distinguish from "productivity measurement" through time; but, as our final section will note, the two traditions can be brought closer together with advantage to a company practicing either. This particular example, reported by Heyworth (1951), the chief officer of Lever Brothers and Unilever, deals with the company's efforts after World War II to improve "efficiency" in terms of output per man-hour and unit cost in soap operations conducted in different countries. Two approaches were taken. First, new "normal" or standard times, lower ones, were sought through changes in "plant layout and equipment," in the "organization of work," and in "human factors." Second, after establishment of the new norms, financial incentives were offered for superior accomplishment.

2.4.2. Capital and Capital-Labor Productivity

The Kendrick-Creamer (1965) handbook already cited describes two cases in which companies have gone beyond labor productivity to capital productivity. One of the companies is Johnson and Johnson; the other is an unnamed "large, multiplant manufacturer" of "durable goods."

The Johnson and Johnson numerator included many individual products, the physical quantities of which were weighted by "standard" costs intended to approximate unit value added. New products were introduced with hypothetical base-year (1950) weights. Composite input embraced "labor, equipment, and machinery, including maintenance," but not structures. Labor input was specifically measured as hours paid, unweighted, rather than hours actually worked. The indicator of capital input was based on the estimated man-hour equivalent of depreciation charges, repairs, and maintenance. Composite labor and capital input was obtained by straight addition, without weights.

The output indicator of the durable-goods producer represented real value added. It was computed by price deflation of (1) sales plus inventory change plus in-house capital additions (2) less purchased materials and services, depreciation, and various taxes. Labor input was measured by unweighted man-hours worked. Capital input, estimated from accounting data with the aid of external price deflators, reflects annual net investment of the company (plant, equipment, land, inventories, accounts receivable, cash, etc.) restated in base-period dollars. For the combination of inputs, labor was weighted by average base-period compensation per man-hour, and capital was weighted by the base-period pretax rate of return.

A third example, published by Cocks (1974), depicts the experience of Eli Lilly and Company in the decade 1963–1972. Real net output was computed as deflated "net sales" minus the deflated value of purchased goods and services, depreciation, and indirect business taxes. Labor input was measured by hours worked; it omitted man-hour losses due to vacation, accident, sickness, and so forth. Deflated inventories and the deflated value of gross and net stocks of equipment and structures were estimated by elaborate procedures suggested by studies made in the Bureau of Economic Analysis of the U.S. Department of Commerce. For the computation of composite productivity, the labor and capital indexes were combined with weights referring to income shares. Cocks presents additional productivity estimates that include capitalized research and development expenditures as an input.

2.4.3. Productivity Examples Involving Intermediate Input

The serial revolution in crude oil prices that began late in 1973 has given a strong impetus to measurement of productivity with respect to energy. Under the Energy Policy and Conservation Act of 1975, major energy-consuming firms are required to report on their efficiency in energy use twice a year—either directly or through third parties, like trade associations. Publications of the Department of Energy (1978*a*, 1978*b*) show the output indicators to be quite simple, even primitive, as a rule, expressed in numbers of barrels, thousands of square feet, tons, and so forth. Energy input is expressed, as might be expected, in Btu's. Also of interest is the report of an inconclusive symposium on the measurement of public-utility productivity (Balk and Shafritz, 1975).

Much more comprehensive company measures of intermediate-input productivity are illustrated in the Kendrick-Creamer handbook (1965). Two cases are described in which companies could also compute their productivity with respect to labor, capital, and all input combined. One of two firms, "a medium-size manufacturer of machinery and equipment," limits monitoring to a relatively new "machine-motor division" that has good records. The other company in this pair is characterized as a "large mideast [United States] manufacturing company."

The machine-motor division's output is based on sales plus inventory change deflated by a company index of catalogue prices. Labor input is represented by hours worked, with hourly rated and salaried workers separately weighted. Capital is estimated as an aggregate of gross fixed assets (land, buildings, and machinery), inventories, cash and marketable securities, notes and accounts receivable, and miscellaneous assets revalued in base-year prices. Intermediate input, represented by raw materials and supplies, purchased services, and depreciation were deflated by in-house and extramural price indexes. A composite productivity measure was computed for all inputs combined. The compiled information also allowed computation of net output and the relation of this output to labor and capital combined.

The "large" manufacturing company's output is represented by deflated "net sales and other operating revenue." Instead of adjustment of this numerator to include inventory change, it was decided to exclude the corresponding input from the denominator. Labor input was estimated as the quotient of total and average hourly compensation. Force-account construction workers were omitted, however, since they were not represented in the output measure. (Research workers should also have been excluded from labor input, but segregation of their earnings was not practicable.) Current dollars of intermediate input—that is, of purchased materials and services—were estimated by deduction of labor compensation and state income taxes from cost of goods sold, and so forth. These estimates were corrected for inventory change, grouped into categories, and deflated by prices deemed appropriate. Depreciation is treated as part of return to capital rather than as an intermediate input. Capital is measured gross, rather than net, in constant dollars. In addition to gross plant and equipment, capital here includes inventories, accounts receivable, cash, securities, and deferred charges. Again, it was possible to compute a productivity measure from net sales and all inputs combined and to derive another measure relating real value added to a labor-capital denominator.

A paper by Craig and Harris (1973), based on a joint prize-winning thesis, provides a third instance in which intermediate input is viewed as coordinate with labor and capital. This example concerns a "relatively large, multi-plant manufacturing company" primarily making "automobile and truck components." Output is represented by deflated values of sales adjusted for inventory changes. Labor input is estimated in base-year dollars of remuneration of wage and salaried workers; it takes account of vacation pay, fringe benefits, and bonuses. Intermediate input includes purchases of raw materials, parts, utilities, and business services (adjusted for inventory change to reflect consumption in the productive process), and all taxes (even federal income taxes). By deflation, all the intermediate categories were restated in base-year dollars. The estimate for capital input is unique—"the sum of annuity values calculated for each asset [buildings, land, equipment, inventories, accounts receivable, and cash] on the basis of its base-year cost, productive life, and the firm's cost of capital."

2.5. SUMMARY AND OUTLOOK

This review has been dominated by the prospect that many more companies, including those providing services, will feel obliged to adopt formal programs of productivity monitoring. Adverse economic circumstances—a persisting high rate of inflation, the uncontrollable price of crude-oil imports, and intense international competition for markets—will commend such monitoring in the interest of company survival and profitability.

As the new wave of productivity monitoring swells, high technical standards should be kept in view. Even when they cannot be honored in the design and construction of actual systems, they offer guidance for evaluation, for reasonable application of the generated numbers, and for future modifications that may become practicable. Accordingly, firms that venture into productivity measurement should at least recognize the desirability of the following:

1. Estimating both output and input in "real" terms—as "quantities" free of price (and other) "noise";
2. Distinguishing between the "verbal" algebra of dimension and the more demanding "literal" algebra of content and structure;
3. Using the easy indirect technique of "deflation" with circumspection;
4. Interpreting productivity figures, not by label, but in the light of the data and methods used in their derivation.

"Partial" productivity measurement will most probably remain the rule, with labor input the favorite denominator as in the past. Companies will surely devote more attention than in the past, however, to intermediate inputs, especially energy and critical materials.

Difficulties of conceptualization and satisfactory measurement of capital will continue to impede the design and construction of comprehensive multi-input monitoring systems. Instead of making ritualistic, imitative measures of capital input anyway, a company would do well to proceed incrementally. Thus, it might realistically do the following:

1. Start with a labor denominator;
2. Develop experience in the use of a labor-productivity measure for a variety of purposes, including investment decisions;
3. Acquire a needed familiarity with concepts, literature, and examples pertaining to company measurement of capital input;
4. Proceed to measure energy productivity if not ready for dealing with capital input.

A traditional belief that output of services cannot be adequately measured—already weakened by gambits in the government sector—will be challenged more energetically as private firms become more fully committed to monitoring. Important additional progress could be achieved by a shift of focus from the measurement of end products to the subproducts that make them up.

The following three frontiers deserve patient exploration by firms that already have in-house measurement programs:

1. The design and construction of measures patterned on the "price" form of the professional productivity definition (this alternative to the usual "quantity" form would seem a natural supplement to conventional accounting);
2. The development and extension of an "atomic" data base that features the compilation of consistent, articulated statistics for company output, input, cost, and price of individual products—or even major subproducts (such integrated statistics would be a boon not only to productivity measurement in accord with the two productivity definitions but also to operational management in general);
3. The closer coordination of the "work measurement" of industrial engineers and managers with the "productivity measurement" of economists, with mutual advantage to both disciplines as well as benefit to company practice (this convergence requires, first, dynamization of the static concept of "efficiency" that relates "standard" to "actual" hours, or "should-take" to "did-take" times, and, second, displacement of primary emphasis from end products to subproducts in productivity measurement).

History has already shown that imperfect measurement is inevitable and can also be useful. It also offers little hope that a foolproof system of quantitative control will ever be devised; or if one is, the scope and applicability will be as great as intended or at first imagined. Accordingly, a leavening of common sense is always desirable in human systems, and supplemental narrative information should not be disparaged. The literal understanding of what a measurement says can help to overcome its limitations in actual use. In particular, even crude productivity indicators can advance productivity performance, especially if their shortcomings are recognized and acknowledged, if their progressive improvement is sought, and if efforts are made to compensate in analysis and interpretation for defects of the numbers themselves.

REFERENCES

Balk, W. L., and J. M. Shafritz, eds., 1975, *Public Utility Productivity: Management and Measurement,* Albany: New York State Department of Public Service (August).

Bernolak, Imre, "Enhancement of Productivity through Interfirm Comparison, a Canadian Experience," in National Center for Productivity and Quality of Working Life, 1976, pp. 59–65.

Carr, Joseph J., 1973, "Measuring Productivity," *Arthur Andersen Chronicle* 33, no. 2:8–18.

Cocks, Douglas L., 1974, "The Measurement of Total Factor Productivity for a Large U.S. Manufacturing Corporation," *Business Economics* 9, no. 4:7–20.

Craig, Charles E., and R. Clark Harris, 1973, "Total Productivity Measurement at the Firm Level," *Sloan Management Review* 14, no. 3:13–29.

Financial Accounting Standards Board, 1979, "Statement of Financial Accounting Standard, No. 33: Financial Reporting and Changing Prices," Stamford, Conn. (September).

Gantz, Marvin E., Jr., 1976, "Productivity Measurement at Alcoa," in National Center for Productivity and Quality of Working Life, 1976, pp. 3, 44.

Greenberg, Leon, 1973, *A Practical Guide to Productivity Measurement,* Washington, D.C.: Bureau of National Affairs.

Heyworth, Geoffrey, 1951, "Productivity," *Advanced Management* 16, no. 3:14–18.

Joint Financial Management Improvement Program, 1977, *Implementing a Productivity Program: Points to Consider,* Washington, D.C.: Gov't. Printing Office (March).

Kendrick, John W., and Daniel Creamer, 1965. *Measuring Company Productivity,* New York: Conference Board.

Klotz, Benjamin, Rey Madoo, and Reed Hansen, 1980, "A Study of High and Low 'Labor Productivity' in U.S. Manufacturing," in J. W. Kendrick and B. N. Vaccara, eds., *New Developments in Productivity Measurement,* Chicago: University of Chicago Press.

Kraus, Jerome, 1978, "Productivity and Profit Models of the Firm," *Business Economics* 13, no. 4:10–14.

Mark, Jerome A., and Charles W. Ardolini, 1974, "Developments in Measuring Productivity in the Federal Sector," in *1974 Proceedings of the Business and Economic Statistics Section, American Statistical Association,* pp. 236–45.

Moore, Brian, 1975, *A Plant-Wide Productivity Plan in Action: Three Years of Experience with the Scanlon Plan,* Washington, D.C.: National Commission on Productivity and Work Quality (May).

National Center for Productivity and Quality of Working Life, 1975, *Improving Productivity: A Description of Selected Company Programs,* Series 1, Washington, D.C.: Gov't. Printing Office (December).

______, 1976, *Improving Productivity through Industry and Company Measurement,* Series 2, Washington, D.C.: Gov't. Printing Office (October).

Panel to Review Productivity Statistics, 1979, *Measurement and Interpretation of Productivity,* Washington, D.C.: National Academy of Sciences.

Peck, Gerald E., 1976, "Measurement of Warehousing Productivity," in National Center for Productivity and Quality of Working Life, 1976, pp. 47–58.

Pratten, C. F., 1976*a*, *A Comparison of the Performance of Swedish and U.K. Companies,* Cambridge: Cambridge University Press.

______, 1976*b*, *Labour Productivity Differentials within International Companies,* Cambridge: Cambridge University Press.

Sherrard, William R., 1967, "Labor Productivity for the Firm," *Quarterly Review of Economics and Business* 7, no. 1:49–61.

Siegel, Irving H., 1976, "Measurement of Company Productivity," in National Center for Productivity and Quality of Working Life, 1976, pp. 15–26.

______, 1980*a*, *Company Productivity: Measurement for Improvement,* Kalamazoo, Mich.: W. E. Upjohn Institute for Employment Research (April).

______, 1980*b*, "Comments on Klotz-Hansen-Madoo Paper," in *New Developments in Productivity Measurement,* Chicago: University of Chicago Press.

U.S. Civil Service Commission, General Accounting Office and Office of Management and Budget, 1972, *Measuring and Enhancing Productivity in the Federal Sector,* Joint Economic Committee, U.S. Congress (August 4).

U.S. Department of Energy, 1978*a*, *Voluntary Business Energy Conservation Program,* Progress Report No. 6, Washington, D.C.: Gov't. Printing Office (April).

______, 1978*b*, *Annual Report: Industrial Energy Efficiency Program,* 2 vols., Washington, D.C.: Gov't. Printing Office (June).

3 MEASUREMENT OF PRODUCTIVITY: *Some Open Issues*

John E. Ullmann

3.1. A TIME OF TROUBLES

The measurement of productivity has now become an essential element in the ongoing and difficult debate on how to improve it. A rising trend in productivity has been a central characteristic of the development of modern industrial society, the organization of its productive systems, the expectations of its citizens, and its patterns of consumption. As Kendrick and Pech (1961, p. 1) aptly put it, "The story of productivity, the ratio of output to input, is at heart the record of man's efforts to raise himself from poverty." It follows that a sustained period of faltering in this improvement process, indeed of a net decline, must necessarily have calamitous consequences for the economy and ultimately the structure, well-being, and cohesion of society.

The most obvious dysfunction is the link between productivity and inflation. In earlier times, a sustained rise in productivity had enabled industry to absorb an ever rising level of real wages and, in many areas, to sustain steady declines in the prices of goods in current or even constant dollars. In the absence of rising productivity, managements pass along in higher prices any increases in wages and other costs. When entire industries go into such a decline, there is no longer any reason for individual companies to hold the line on prices. As Hong (1979) has shown, stagflation is the result; inflation, stagnation of markets and profits, and rising unemployment exist together.

Pressures also rise toward cost cutting, efficiencies, and other changes, and major sociopolitical arrangements of the last several decades get called into question. In 1978, an attempt to make some minor changes in the labor laws triggered a particularly protracted and violent filibuster in the U.S. Senate and the bill was lost. Its defeat was accompanied at the time by a new political aggressiveness on the part of business lobbies, notably such new organizations as the Committee on a Union-Free Environment, under the auspices of the National Association of Manufacturers. In a Labor Day speech, Secretary of Labor Ray Marshall (1978) described what had happened: "Suddenly we were no longer debating labor law reform. Instead, we were refighting the basic battles over unions, collective bargaining and industrial democracy that we believed had been settled during the 1930's."

Since that time, to cite but a few examples, unemployment compensation was made partly subject to income tax to provide "incentives" for recipients to take other jobs (any jobs), and the minimum wage came under sustained attack once again. The authority of the Federal Trade Commission was circumscribed by funding holdups and congressional vetoes over its decisions. All such efforts have their effects on productivity; they change either the inputs (at least in dollars) or the outputs (product quality, for instance) in the basic productivity fraction. A slight contrary trend was evidenced in the U.S. Supreme Court decision in *Whirlpool Corp.* v. *Marshall,* No. 78–1870, in which workers were given greater latitude in refusing to do dangerous jobs. Whether this will significantly affect the work of such organizations as Stop OSHA, funded by the U.S. Chamber of Commerce, remains to be seen.

In fine, what is involved here is a protracted struggle inside all industrial societies, for the issues have been joined outside the United States as well, including, for example, within the Soviet bloc. What is at stake is quite plainly who will pay for the troubled times ahead, that is, what portions of society will have their interests most adversely affected.

Under these conditions, the way in which productivity is to be measured takes on substantial importance. What is measured and how it is measured helps to determine the results; method determines substance, instead of being more or less independent. It is then a rather futile task to set as an objective for productivity measurement, the kind of single goal a physical scientist might set in other problems of mensuration; to the contrary, a multiplicity of measures may well be in order, with a sharp awareness of the distinctions between them. In what follows, some basic methodological problems are first briefly discussed, followed by a review of some current issues in the measurements of inputs and then of outputs in economic activities. The quality as well as quantity of change is the basic problem. Finally, social value judgments must enter into the equation as well, especially in the area of services that form a particularly difficult part of productivity measurement.

3.2. METHODOLOGICAL ISSUE: CAUSALITY

As discussed in the previous chapter by Siegel, there are many approaches to productivity analysis covered in the literature.

Gold (1955); Eilon, Gold, and Soesan (1976); Kendrick (1977); Heaton (1977); Greenberg (1973); and Hornbruch (1977) are some of the works that, in varying proportions, cover problems of measurement and suggestions for improvement, dealing with the problem both within organizations and within society at large. The works sometimes may be prescriptive as well as descriptive. Inevitably, this can raise basic questions as to how much causal relationship there is between inputs and outputs and between productivity measures and other societal variables. In such a methodological environment it may even become a central objective to show that virtually everything is somebody's fault or to somebody's credit.

It is thus well to note the cautionary point made by Mills (1955, pp. 502–03) that "measures of productivity carry no causal imputation; services of land, capital, labor etc. do not necessarily determine the output or the efficiency" with which it is produced. Causality may be shared in many ways not necessarily observable from productivity ratios. As Mills says:

> It is convenient and meaningful to measure changes in output with reference to changes in some one component of the factor composite, but it would be a great mistake to assume that this factor operates alone in bringing about a gain or loss. In general, . . . it is most useful to measure output with reference to the input of human effort. . . . But we must recognize that the effectiveness of this effort varies not alone with the intensity and skill of the human factor, but also with the number and quality of the tools employed, the amount of power utilized, the nature of the productive organization, and other features of the productive process.

When, in the face of such difficulties, specific reasons are ascribed to changes in productivity, the results become rather, shall one say, sensitive. For example, in one widely noted recent study, Denison (1978) concluded:

> By 1975, . . . output per unit of input in the non-residential business sector of the economy was 1.8% smaller than it would have been if business had operated

under 1967 conditions. Of this amount, 1.0% is ascribable to pollution abatement and 0.4% each to employee safety and health programs and to the increase in dishonesty and crime.

Denison added a carefully phrased disclaimer: "The purpose of this article is to aid analysis of growth and productivity; it is not to judge the wisdom of government programs which have benefits as well as costs." This disclaimer has been ignored by many of those quoting Denison's findings in the current antiregulation controversies. The cost of compliance with regulations does form part of the inputs or outputs in the productivity equation, but so do the benefits. It could equally be argued that what has happened in the latest extensions of regulatory scope is merely more of the replacement of what had been social costs by business costs. And that is a phenomenon as old as the embodiment of weights and measures standards in the Code of Hammurabi. In the present American context, we may well be running some sort of "profit" on regulations, but that in turn would require us to measure items not easily quantified, a point that will be further addressed below.

In a later study, Denison (1979) reviewed the literature of productivity analysis; he considered over one hundred different sources and pointed to the large unexplainable residual. He suggested that "it is possible, perhaps even probable, that everything went wrong at once among the determinants that affect the residual series" after the main effects had been considered. He expressed the hope that the expiration of time, yielding more data, will allow a more decisive explanation. Certainly such widely accepted factors as the decline in innovation must be counted as significant negative influences; some other considerations are discussed elsewhere in this chapter. A simplistic identification of "regulations" as the main culprit masks a good deal of managerial incompetence (Ullmann, 1980*b*).

3.3. LABOR INPUTS

Labor productivity is the statistic most frequently collected; it is the subject matter of the regular series of productivity statistics collected by the Bureau of Labor Statistics (BLS, 1978). It is usually presented as indexes of output per employee hour (formerly man-hour, and *that* also was a significant issue not long ago) of production workers and of all employees.

The controversies in these measures concern (1) the extent to which labor, of whatever kind, is responsible for its performance; (2) the relevance of the once quite sharp division between production workers and others; and (3) the division between workers and managements of the benefits of improvement in processes and management. The latter is involved whenever the issue of productivity comes up in labor negotiations. In general, the interpretation of these issues depends on whether the job is worker paced, machine paced, demand paced or material paced. The latter is encountered in the processing of natural resources but also, as will be noted later, in some services.

One example concerns the shift from worker-paced skilled machining to numerically controlled and thus substantially more machine-paced work. Further, this development affected the division between production workers and others in that the jobs once done on the shop floor were moved to the office. Thus, the use of computer numerical controls (CNC) led to the transfer of the setup function from the machinists to computer programmers who (not coincidentally) were office people and thus not members of the shop union. The CNC replaced the "record and play back" method that, inter alia, provided the inspiration for Kurt Vonnegut's *Player Piano* (1952); Vonnegut had worked on the design of the equipment. Noble (1979) has provided an account of the attempt by the shop workers to recapture some control over the work pace. Some of the tactics included watching with equanimity as a wrongly programmed machine damaged itself in trying to follow orders. Eventually, the value of manual overrides had to be recognized and the workers more directly involved in the programming function. To the extent that such problems diminish the productivity gains of such equipment, they would further add deterrents to its use, although the biggest one is still its high price (see De Luca, 1980).

The details of the above incident should not obscure the important point that categories of labor can be substantially manipulated and thus differences in the productivity of production and other employees must be viewed with considerable care. A parallel set of problems is posed by the practice of the BLS in classifying workers in some industries as supervisory and nonsupervisory.

The CNC example also suggests that the improvement of productivity has not inevitably led to a replacement of worker-paced by machine-paced operations, though, of course, this has often happened. As Melman (1957) showed, workers are not entirely helpless in deciding their work pace even in highly automated and therefore machine-paced operations. The human limits to machine pacing were demonstrated also by the Lordstown (Ohio) strikes.

But an even more fundamental change is at work in some industries. Conventionally organized groups of workers led by foremen of the traditional stripe become unnecessary and are replaced by individuals having a fair degree of autonomy. This happens when work primarily consists of maintenance requiring few workers, mostly alone or in very small units.

This change has been a major factor in the decline in worker-hours per unit of output in several industries such as oil refining or public utilities (see, for instance, Estcourt, 1955).

Another recent development related to the boundary between worker- and machine-paced operations is worthy of note. It has been suggested that the higher cost of energy will force a reversal of a long trend in which energy-using equipment is substituted for manual labor. Forecasts of this sort have been made part of the gloomy assessments of our future that have become fashionable—what one might call the "more-hard-work-for-our-sins" approach.

It is correct that the terms of trade between energy and labor have changed. For much of this century, the number of kilowatt-hours that one hour of hourly earnings in manufacturing would buy showed a rising trend, from 39 in 1924, to 59 in 1937, to 158 in 1950, to a high of 286 in 1967. Since then, the ratio has fallen to 223 in 1977, recovering somewhat to 245 by November 1979. Still, the time of growth in this ratio seems to be over (Melman, 1956, p. 213; Ullmann, 1980*a*, pp. 14, 310; Bureau of Labor Statistics, 1980, pp. 80, 94).

Before one applies these statistics to the new substitution problem, however, one must distinguish between a literal substitution of labor for energy in a given operation and the general and rather obvious point that with energy costs rising, more investments and business activities (including labor inputs) can be justified on the basis that they save energy. The former category is, in fact, most unlikely to have a serious impact. The reason is that the work heads—what one might call the business end—of machines were generally mechanized decades ago. A further major improvement in labor productivity came as the result of more mechanized materials-handling equipment in the period 1930–1950. After that it was mostly in the area of controls that, though always important to a certain extent, experienced a quantum jump in sophistication as a result of progress in electronics, which in turn was soon to be dominated by solid state devices and computers. These, on the other hand, use very little power themselves. One can hardly justify putting brawn back to work on the basis of energy saving alone, if there is an otherwise cost-effective (i.e., not too expensive) control system available.

Next, new problems have arisen in allocating responsibility for worker performance. Unless the job is truly worker paced, it is not an easy concept to define fairly. For example, in many areas of the United States, substantial efforts are being made to hold teachers "accountable" for the performance of their students. Yet teaching is perhaps one of the most material-paced activities, certainly among services. The receptivity of students to instruction is determined by a multiplicity of cultural, socioeconomic, and sometimes religious or political influences outside the school. Similarly, the performance of a local health service depends quite obviously on the general state of health of the population, which is in turn affected, if not determined, by such societal factors.

Similar problems in the allocation and distribution of labor input occur in such demand-paced activities as, for instance, retailing. To the extent that salespeople are provided (sometimes on commission), they should be able to offer service and advice to prospective buyers, *whenever they show up*. Whether any actually do, however, is a result of managerial decisions on location, buying, pricing, advertising, decor, and so forth over which the sales force on the floor has virtually no control.

In both material-paced and demand-paced services, one response has been to lower the service level until everybody is busy all the time. In the parlance of the theory of waiting lines, the channel utilization ratio is pushed to near 1 if not to more than 1; in the latter case, the queue keeps on increasing until admissions are stopped, after which the accumulated customers are serviced (for an example, see Ullmann, 1976, p. 330).

An even more pervasive approach to cutting the labor input and thus improving productivity is to increase the proportion of self-service; so far, at least, it has probably had a greater effect than such technical innovations as computer-related equipment. Retailing furnishes the most obvious examples, but do-it-yourself medicine, for example, is also making an appearance. In 1979, the sustained growth of eating out, especially in fast-food establishments, slowed down considerably. At least one supermarket chain in the New York area attempted to ride the trend by advising its customers by radio commercial to adopt a new cost-saving strategy—cooking at home. Do-it-yourself is advocated once again; social historians might be interested in trends that for a long time had propelled individuals into ever more technically sophisticated activities in home construction, for instance, while relegating cooking, surely one of the most ancient of personal activities, to something to be performed as a service by outsiders.

Finally, there is the question of the division of the benefits that labor and management bring to an enterprise. In an industrial context, the issue is at least as old as the scientific management school founded by Frederick W. Taylor in the 1880s. Taylor's critics, often with the benefit of rather long hindsight, point out that he tended to look upon workers as outer-directed brutes requiring a strong hand and that his view of workers as cogs in the machine dehumanized them. He also believed that value judgments could be quantified, a view still shared by some in the social sciences, the operations researchers and others. Nevertheless, Taylor was more generous in allocating the workers' share of the proceeds than some contemporaries, such as Henry Gantt, who took exception to much of Taylor's ideology on humanist grounds (Gomberg, 1955, pp. 1126–128).

Drucker (1974, p. 188) defines the issues as follows:

> There is no resolution to this conflict. One has to live with it. Work is a living for the worker. . . . But work also produces the capital for the economy. It produces the means by which an economy perpetuates itself, provides for the risks of economic activity and the resources of tomorrow. . . . There is need in any economy for a wage fund and for a capital fund.

The capital fund has undoubtedly helped provide much of the equipment and investment required to produce in turn steadily rising real wages for as long as the productivity gains could sustain them. Drucker notes, however (p. 189), that the capital formed in one industry often was invested in another and that gains and sacrifices differ sharply among different kinds of workers. Here, Drucker's distinction between manual workers and what he terms knowledge workers is important. Clearly, the latter group has increased sharply in size and power and thus obtained a rising share of the wage fund. The question of how much good this increase in nonproduction workers contributes then becomes central to whatever resolution is proposed to the conflict over the funds. The "output" of management will be further discussed in a later section.

3.4. CAPITAL INPUTS

Capital inputs are generally defined as

CI = (invested capital at beginning of year) + (additions, i.e., new investments in the year) − (depreciation for the year).

As Greenberg (1973, p. 51) says, "the value of capital is measured in accordance with the company's accounting practices . . . usually in terms of replacement costs." But that is exactly where a major problem lies. Replacement cost accounting is not standard at all, mainly because it conflicts with accounting practice for tax computations. There are also substantial variations in other aspects of accounting procedures.

The leading problem with CI as defined above is, however, that the numbers are manipulable to a very considerable extent. The use of other than straight-line depreciation, various provisions for rapid write-off of certain assets, and accounting carry-overs have made the annual additions and subtractions to CI a regulated rather than fixed item, and the first term in the equation is itself the product of years of such often rather dubious practice.

The amount of invested capital may also be inflated or understated because of prior reorganizations, mergers, and even bankruptcies; it may be no indication of the utility of production facilities because these may be (and not infrequently are) quite old and thus no longer carried on the books. Yet they clunk, chug, or grind away day after day and clearly fulfill a viable function. The investment credits and rapid write-offs have further contributed to this pool of useful but "zero" capital.

As to the annual new investment, this may be grossly distorted by the contractual or bookkeeping details of what was paid for and when it was paid for. This is a point especially to be considered when lead times are long as they are these days for almost everything in industrial equipment. Furthermore, as mergers and horizontal integration continue, facilities in an industry may be concentrated in ever fewer establishments. A major expansion may then throw off the statistics quite substantially and one may have to resort to a kind of "income averaging"—but this also is not always readily possible and may be somewhat artificial anyway.

Nevertheless, capital productivity is clearly an important factor. Without going into extensive detail, we can see by the gradual aging of American machinery that something obviously is wrong with the economics of new equipment. A recent study (Ullmann, 1980*a*) showed extensive declines in productivity or at least stagnation in many industries, with the literature often noting that some "innovations" were available but cost too much for the benefits they might bring. All this, of course, further adds to the stock of capital equipment that shows up as zero in the statistics. Even if one would say that this equipment does not matter, there would still be a changing effect over time that would be most inaccurate to ignore.

Furthermore, the quality of investment again becomes an issue. Denison (1978) distinguishes between "productive" and "defensive" investment, the latter reserved for items needed for environmental or safety devices in the process and for the safety aspects of the product itself. But such classifications are bound to become arbitrary and most certainly self-serving. For example, some eighty years ago, the copper industry had to switch from oxide to sulfide ores; nobody would have called that defensive in Denison's sense, though one might certainly describe it thus. It did, after all, save the industry's future. Also, the industry has long recovered several rare metals from its flue dust; it is the only commercial source of some of them. Yet putting in a new precipitator might well be called defensive because its main purpose is pollution abatement.

Clearly, a good measure of capital productivity would be very useful in industrial planning. However, the above problems have led to measures that often show violent swings little related to any observable change in the fortunes of the industry. Some of the series are, in any event, only collected at rare intervals, as in the Census of Manufactures, and then the release of the data is delayed for years. The 1977 census was not yet fully published in 1980.

There is no easy answer to these problems. Proposals for counting only productive equipment would be difficult to put into practice, especially for intra-industry, let alone inter-industry, comparisons (Greenberg, 1973, p. 52). Gold (in Eilon, Gold, and Soesan, 1976, pp. 22–23) has proposed various measures for stating capital productivity simply as profit on investment. This is proper for a single firm but, again, subject to the variations detailed above.

There is one further aspect of the quality of capital investment. It is the effect and role of economy of scale. It is not to be confused with capacity of an industry, which is what economists generally use when attempting to factor it in (see, for instance, Denison, 1974, and Kendrick, 1973; for a discussion of the difference between the two measures, see Gold, 1955). A study directed by the writer (Ullmann, 1980*a*) discusses the effects of economy of scale in particular industries and their equipment and concludes that a major part of technical progress in fact consists of making equipment bigger rather than qualitatively different and presumably better. Size pays; it costs no more to push the start button on a large automatic machine than on a small one.

But reliance on making things ever larger is not a viable option in the long run. Empirical studies indicate that economy of scale is governed by the relationship

$$C = aK^b,$$

where C is the total cost of the plant, K its capacity in units, and a and b are constants, with $b < 1$, whenever economy of scale is present. Cost per unit of capacity is then given by

$$U = \frac{C}{K} = aK^{b-1}.$$

This relationship is a mathematical parallel to the learning curve. If one then postulates a learning fraction p, such that every doubling of K leads to a reduction of U to p times its former value, then it can be shown (see Ullmann, 1976, pp. 3–7, for details) that

$$p = 2^{b-1}.$$

This means that every time a reduction of magnitude p is desired, the capacity must be doubled, and clearly this cannot go on indefinitely. One must add to these mathematical limitations major market disturbances, for example, those due to such demographic changes as an aging population or to market segmentation in which large physical volumes must be split among a varied product line, thus inhibiting the realization of economy of scale.

Such problems in the quality and measurement of investment make a productivity measure of the resources fed into the system per unit of time a goal that has not yet been convincingly achieved.

3.5. OUTPUT OF PRODUCTS

The standard methods of computing a quantity index are well known and given in most statistics texts (see, for instance, Mills, 1955, p. 489). The weighting of the quantity entries is done by price. It has recently been suggested that in very heterogeneous industries such as construction, this method may lead to erroneous results because price indexes are difficult to compute (see the report in *Business Week,* 1980). However, the critics also point to rapidly changing outputs of the industry and there lies one of the main measurement problems. What bothered the critics of the productivity indexes of the construction industry was that the labor index had risen from 58 in 1949 to 103 in 1968 (1967 = 100), only to fall to an estimated 71 in 1979, that is, back to the level of 1953. This the industry is reluctant to believe, but one's own observations of cost and time overruns in construction projects lend at least anecdotal confirmation to a significant decline.

At any rate, product change is a major disturbing factor. Consider first the routine efforts by manufacturers and their engineers to cut the manufacturing costs of products. There is nothing unseemly about this per se—quite the contrary—but if this is done by the recognized and quite respectable precepts of value analysis, it means "omit, combine, make cheaper." It is in fact one of the criticisms of modern engineering education that under pressure from space age, or rather weapons age, technology, engineers are no longer taught enough about producibility and commercial development in general. They then have to be second-guessed by specialists in value analysis (Ullmann and Gluck, 1980, p. 22).

However they are made, any such changes affect productivity even if the customer gets a functionally equivalent or possibly even superior product. From the viewpoint of social need, the same need has been met, but clearly the improvement of productivity recorded is not relevant to the measurement of work load or to collective bargaining controversies, unless again the matter is reduced to the effects on individual operations.

Substitutions of materials, for example, plastics for metals, also lead to great changes. Not only may whole departments become obsolescent or be gradually phased out, but the firm may decide to buy rather than make. Its output, insofar as it is a function of value added by manufacture, shows a decline. In all of this there is the further issue that research may on one hand be capitalized and thus show up in that rather vague item called capital input or may be paid for as a separate contract with some outside agency.

While such changes may be the result of extensive technical effort, others may be based on a managerial judgment of what the company can get away with. It is the increasing prevalence of products for which, in the words of the small print in the TV commercials, "some assembly is required." What better way of reducing labor than by having the customer do the job! Of course, sometimes the customers are not exactly willing. There is a long history of trouble in the auto industry arising from cars so incompletely assembled that dealers call them do-it-yourself kits. The dealers then have to assemble them as part of their "dealer-prep" work for which the customers are charged an increasingly handsome fee. Even at that the dealers complain about being insufficiently compensated. There is need for some real studies of how much of the productivity gains in various areas is due precisely to this "laying off" of what had at one time been very much a part of the process of making the product concerned.

It is also something of a myth to assume that better safety has led to a substantial increase in the work required to produce most products. Few measures are more stoutly resisted by industry than those requiring extra safety features; to the contrary, as of 1980, industry was making an effort to have negligence suits against it made more difficult (Witt, 1980). The writer analyzed automobile features likely to improve safety in 1962 and concluded that the automobile industry tended to make mainly changes that would reduce manufacturing costs. Safety features, if cost increasing, were only used when legally required. At that time, the industry even opposed mandatory seat belts (Ullmann, 1962, pp. 248–64).

There is a basic conflict between measures that simply take the product as given at any time and those that actually attempt to hold the product constant in order to have the productivity ratio truly measure differences in effort required over time. Such attempts, however, have generally not been too successful except when applied on an operation-by-operation basis; they then become a simple extension of work measurement. When attempts have been made to apply that kind of constant output criterion to broader product lines, the effort has turned out to be both expensive and of only ephemeral importance; products changed and made the carefully collected data obsolete.

One of the most extensive studies in the United States was the series of monographs on productivity and factory performance on a few products that the Bureau of Labor Statistics (1951–1954) prepared for the Industrial and Technical Assistance Division of the Foreign Operations Administration (the name of the foreign aid program at the time). The data, collected in great detail, did not retain their importance for long.

One of the studies, for instance, concerned five-horsepower induction motors that, while not the kind of homogeneous bulk material that makes the measurement of output easy, are a well-standardized product. Their dimensions and output particulars are set by the National Electrical Manufacturers Association (NEMA) in order to make the motors interchangeable. The study was done in 1954; however, beginning in 1958, the industry converted to a new standard because of great improvements in aluminum die casting (for the rotors), magnetic steels, and insulation. These allowed the motors to shrink two standard sizes for a given output; a five-horsepower motor was made about the same size as a two-horsepower motor had been, a change that realized a great saving not only in materials but also in manufacturing productivity, in that a physically much smaller unit took much less effort to make. It was a demonstration of the role of cost reduction as a key criterion of design change (Ullmann, 1959).

Such possibilities in which a great improvement in cost effectiveness was made without impairing the function of the product depend on a substantial flow of innovation and that has also drastically slowed down. The role of the slowdown in innovation in calling into question the very industrial future of the United States is well acknowledged in current writings on productivity. Dumas (1979), Melman (1974), and Ullmann (1978*a*) have traced the problem to the misapplication of technology and investment capital to military purposes in which very little is actually contributed to the commercial viability of U.S. manufacturing industry.

3.6. OUTPUT OF SERVICES

It is almost tautological to say that the output of services is very difficult to measure. The sources of the difficulty, however, are less often discussed. It was pointed out earlier that many services are demand paced, so that productivity improvement of a sort is possible by making people wait and having fewer service channels. Just as a polluting and unsafe plant in a real sense has a free ride on the health of its neighbors and its workers, so a highly "productive" service of this kind has a free ride on the time of those waiting. As John Milton said, "They also serve who only stand and wait";

and that quite often includes the clients of retail clerks, repair mechanics, maintenance staffs, and government officials of all kinds. Bureaucracies, as Blau and Meyer (1971) have carefully demonstrated, were originally established to introduce some regularity into governmental decisions that had previously been made on an ad hoc basis by local lords. Still, there is the problem of defining what service they render.

If that question is to be answered by reference to the old definition of services as the human care of human beings, the justification of much of what passes as service is indeed tenuous. Rather, one might perhaps do better by considering instead the First Law of Thermodynamics by which an energy input δE is split into an output component of useful work δW and a component of internal energy δI, that is,

$$\delta E = \delta W + \delta I,$$

where δI, in the present context, means internal churning about, without really "serving" anybody or anything in any significant form.

The extent of these nonactivities is often shown by looking at the linkages between the department whose productivity is to be studied and the service the entire organization is supposed to perform. This does not mean that anything other than direct labor does not count as a fruitful input, but it does suggest that the output deserves careful examination. C. N. Parkinson (1962, Chap. 1) tells of the disappearance of his work load in an army office in World War II, as soon as his two colleagues went on leave. It turned out that they had spent most of their time sending each other memos. Yet such internal measures of output are often proposed as indicators of productivity; most of the time, the proponents recognize their inadequacy, but they are better than nothing. The public sector also includes many direct services, such as nationalized transport enterprises, sewers and water supply, garbage collection, public education, and so forth that, from an operational viewpoint have quasi-manufacturing characteristics. For instance, they are not demand paced in the sense that personal or business services are. Rather, they are ultimately delimited by market influences resembling those portions of the private sector that supply the more obvious necessities of life. The effects of a given service on public well-being are not always clear, as was noted earlier in the cases of health and education, but the products of the manufacturing sector are not often asked to meet such tests either.

Rather than lump services together, therefore, it may be more helpful in the future to focus on the overhead function in general. Much of the staff work in larger organizations may turn out to be as full of δI as Parkinson's job. Value analysis, based on the bottom line of ultimate service, may well be very much in order. It may be objected that some of the modern staff functions are mandated by government regulations; these too might be cut, however, if more attention were focused on a modus vivendi, rather than on spending much of the effort in fighting the government. Certainly, there are enough reasons for worrying about the growth and proliferation of overhead functions (for a set of case studies, see Ullmann, 1978*b* and 1980*b*).

3.7. VALUE JUDGMENTS

The measurement of productivity ultimately raises the question of what a given society desires to do with its resources. Just as in the measurement of capital inputs, some writers on the problem have advocated only measuring productive equipment, so a society should also pay attention to what can be called productive in a broader social sense. It would certainly be possible to argue that insofar as efficiency in the use of resources is a desirable social goal, the real effort should lie in reducing activities that add to what one might call the overhead of society, rather than supplying its needs and contributing to its well-being.

Such critical views of what is considered productive must necessarily apply to all the various instruments of oppression that modern governments have fashioned for themselves. The connection between these and industry is often uncomfortably close. After all, firms successful in making steel-mill and foundry equipment, refractories, and so forth also built the facilities of Auschwitz and Birkenau. Today's national security apparatus contrives to combine the traditional barbarities of its society with new ones, as well as with computers. There is grim potential for improving the internal measures of productivity of such institutions, as well as for what Winston Churchill once called "a new dark age, made darker and more protracted by the lights of perverted science."

Beyond such issues, there are immediate ones concerning the functioning of society. Bearing in mind the above discussion of social overhead and the δI-factor in the contemporary occupational structure, could one not envisage a society in which such activities are reduced?

A proper choice of what a society is to do with its resources is the ultimate value judgment. It involves many variables beyond those discussed here. Most of them are not quantifiable but are still important. Ignoring these determinants of social decisions leads to the following fallacy as Daniel Yankelovich has defined it (quoted in Smith, 1972, p. 286):

> The first step is to measure whatever can be easily measured. This is okay as far as it goes. The second step is to disregard that which can't be measured or give it an arbitrary quantitative value. This is artificial and misleading. The third step is

to presume that what can't be measured easily really isn't very important. This is blindness. The fourth step is to say that what can't be easily measured really doesn't exist. This is suicide.

The answer, then, appears to be to try to acquire a clearer grasp of the limitations of current and of prospective measurements of productivity and to use them with care.

REFERENCES

Blau, Peter M., and Marshall W. Meyer, 1971, *Bureaucracy in Modern Society,* New York: Random House.

Business Week, 1980, "A Productivity Drop That Nobody Believes," February 25, p. 77.

De Luca, John, 1980, "Machine Tools," in Ullmann, (1980*a*, pp. 289–98).

Denison, Edward F., 1974, *Accounting for United States Economic Growth,* Washington, D.C.: Brookings Institution.

———, 1978, "Effects of Selected Changes in the Institutional and Human Environment upon Output per Unit of Input," *Survey of Current Business,"* January:21–44.

———, 1979, "Explanations of Declining Productivity Growth," *Survey of Current Business,* August, Pt. 2:1–24.

Drucker, Peter, 1974, *Management,* New York: Harper & Row.

Dumas, Lloyd J., 1979, "Productivity and the Roots of Stagflation," *Proceedings of the American Institute of Industrial Engineers* (May).

Eilon, Samuel, Bela Gold, and Judith Soesan, 1976, *Applied Productivity Analysis for Industry,* Oxford: Pergamon Press.

Estcourt, V. F., 1955, "Manpower and Other Factors Affecting the Operating Costs of Steam Generating Stations," *Transactions of ASME* 77:343.

Gold, Bela, 1955, *Foundations of Productivity Analysis,* Pittsburgh: University of Pittsburgh Press.

Gomberg, William, 1955, "Trade Unions and Industrial Engineering," in Ireson and Grant, 1955, pp. 1126–28.

Greenberg, Leon, 1973, *A Practical Guide to Productivity Measurement,* Washington, D.C.: Bureau of National Affairs.

Heaton, Herbert, 1977, *Productivity in Service Organizations,* New York: McGraw-Hill.

Hong, B. Y., 1979, *Inflation under Cost Pass-Along Management,* New York: Praeger.

Hornbruch, Frederick W., 1977, *Raising Productivity,* New York: McGraw-Hill.

Ireson, W. G., and E. L. Grant, eds., 1955, *Handbook of Industrial Engineering and Management,* Englewood Cliffs, N.J.: Prentice-Hall.

Kendrick, J. W., 1973, *Postwar Productivity Trends in the United States, 1948–1969,* New York: National Bureau of Economic Research.

______, 1977, *Understanding Productivity,* Baltimore: Johns Hopkins University Press.
Kendrick, J. W., and M. Pech, 1961, *Productivity Trends in the United States,* New York: National Bureau of Economic Research.
Malkiel, Burton G., 1979, "Productivity—the problem behind the Headlines," *Harvard Business Review,* May-June:17-27
Marshall, Ray, 1978, "Double Trouble for Labor," *Newsday,* September 7.
Melman, Seymour, 1956, *Dynamic Factors in Industrial Productivity,* Oxford: Basil Blackwell.
______, 1957, *Decision-Making and Productivity,* Oxford: Basil Blackwell.
______, 1974, *The Permanent War Economy,* New York: Simon & Schuster.
Mills, F. C., 1955, *Statistical Methods,* New York: Henry Holt.
Noble, David F., 1979, "Social Choices in Machine Design," in Andrew Zimbalist, ed., *Case Studies in the Labor Process,* New York: Monthly Review Press.
Orwell, George, 1937, *The Road to Wigan Pier,* London: Gollancz.
Parkinson, C. Northcote, 1962, *The Law and the Profits,* Boston: Houghton-Mifflin.
Smith, Adam [pseud.], 1972, *Supermoney,* New York: Random House.
Ullmann, John E., 1959, "Criteria of Change in Machine Design," Ph.D. dissertation, Columbia University.
______, 1962, "Some Economic Aspects of Automotive Safety Devices," in *Passenger Car Design and Highway Safety,* Mount Vernon, N.Y.: Consumers Union of the U.S.
______, 1976, *Quantitative Methods in Management,* New York: McGraw-Hill.
______, 1978*a,* "Tides and Shallows," in Lewis Benton, ed., *Management for the Future,* New York: McGraw-Hill.
______, 1978*b, Problems in the Growth and Efficiency of Administrative and Service Functions,* Hempstead, N.Y.: Hofstra Yearbooks of Business.
______, ed., 1980*a*, *The Improvement of Productivity,* New York: Praeger.
______, 1980*b*, "See What You Made Me Do," in Lewis Benton, ed., *Private Management and Public Policy,* Lexington, Mass.: Lexington Books.
Ullmann, John E., and Samuel E. Gluck, 1980, *Manufacturing Management,* Columbus, Ohio: Transwin Publishers.
U.S. Bureau of Labor Statistics, 1951-1954, *Case Studies in Productivity and Factory Performance: 5-Horsepower Induction Motors, Diesel Engines, Fractional Horsepower Motors,* Washington, D.C.: Gov't. Printing Office.
______, 1978, *Productivity Indexes in Selected Industries,* Bulletin 2002, Washington, D.C.: Gov't. Printing Office.
______, 1980, "Statistical Supplement," *Monthly Labor Review,* January:80, 94.
Vonnegut, Kurt, 1952, *Player Piano,* New York: Delacorte Press.
Witt, Matt, 1980, "A Design Priority: Safer Machines," *New York Times,* January 29.

4 PRODUCTIVITY MEASUREMENT AT THE LEVEL OF THE FIRM: *An Application within Food Retailing*

Hirotaka Takeuchi

The sluggishness of U.S. productivity growth that has characterized much of the 1970s is of pivotal concern to policymakers. This concern is reflected in the 1979 *Economic Report,* in which "the Carter Administration told Congress . . . that lagging economic productivity had reduced the country's capacity to create more jobs and higher living standards" (*New York Times,* January 26, 1979, p. D1).

Most of this concern is aimed at the macroeconomic levels. At the international level, policymakers are concerned that between 1970 and 1977 the United States recorded the second lowest manufacturing productivity growth rate among eleven industrialized countries, the lowest being the United Kingdom (*Monthly Labor Review,* November 1978, pp. 11–17). At the national level, economic planners are concerned, since "President Carter has identified [productivity] as perhaps the most troublesome underlying cause of inflation" (*New York Times,* January 26, 1979, p. D1). Of particular concern is a recent study conducted by the New York Stock Exchange (1979), which suggests that a small productivity decline may have a large "multiplier" effect on inflation. Policymakers are also concerned, albeit to a lesser extent, with the "causal" influence of productivity on such national issues as unemployment, work ethics, and living standards. At the sector or industry level, policymakers are concerned with certain laggard sectors and industries. The government and service sectors, for example, have been identified as contributing to poor productivity performance at the national level.[1] The food retailing industry, which showed an annual productivity decline of 1.0 percent between 1972 and 1977, is another case in point (*Monthly Labor Review,* September 1978, pp. 54–56).

Policymakers see lagging productivity as endangering continued national prosperity. They are currently frustrated because despite the widespread agreement about the slowdown of U.S. productivity growth, the causes or cures of this slowdown have not been clearly identified.[2] In the words of Charles L. Schultze, chairman of the Council of Economic Advisers, "Unfortunately, there are no magic buttons to push to improve productivity" (*New York Times,* January 26, 1979, p. D3).

Although the "magic buttons" are yet to be found, productivity research at the macro level has progressed from the "dark ages" of the 1950s through the data development stage of the 1960s and onward to the analysis stage of the 1970s. In contrast, productivity research at the micro level (i.e., at the level of the firm or establishment) is still in the "dark ages." A large number of corporate managers still face two basic problems. First of all, they are still unclear about how productivity should be measured. According to a recent article (*New York Times,* January 27, 1979, p. 26), "The largest corporations say they cannot measure [productivity] on their own production lines. Yet government economists can chart it on an economy-wide basis." Second, corporate managers are not yet convinced about the usefulness of productivity indexes as a managerial tool.

Although the two problems are interrelated, this paper will focus on the first of them, the measurement problem. The objective of the paper is to develop and test a new measure of productivity that can be utilized at the level of the firm or establishment. To accomplish this objective, the paper will proceed through the following five steps: (1) describe past measurement approaches at the micro level, (2) present a conceptual basis of the new measure of output, (3) illustrate the methodological steps required to develop the new measure, (4) test the validity of the new measure, and (5) construct partial and total factor productivity indexes based on it.

4.1. MEASUREMENT APPROACHES AT THE MICRO LEVEL

Although the micro level is limited in scope and in depth relative to the macro level, several attempts have been made to measure productivity at the micro level. With no pretense of being comprehensive, this section summarizes five different measurement approaches at the micro level that have appeared in the various literatures.

The first is the "macro-oriented" approach associated with such economists as Kendrick and Creamer (1965), Craig and Harris (1973), Cocks (1974), Gantz (1976), and others. These economists take existing company data and try to apply to them measurement conventions adopted at the macro level. The resulting company measures of productivity, then, become compatible with macro measures based on the national income accounts data, or the Bureau of Labor Statistics data, or both.[3] This enables corporate managers to compare the company's productivity performance with that of the industry or the sector, as demonstrated by Cocks with Eli Lilly and by Gantz with Alcoa.

The second is the "financial" approach espoused by accountants and financial analysts. Productivity measures developed by such researchers as Davis (1955), Gold (1955), and Martin (1964) adhere to conventions followed in cost accounting and finance. On the positive side, measures developed in this manner are easily interpretable by corporate managers and easily constructed through simple recalculation of data in the balance sheet, or profit and loss statements, or both. But on the negative side, there is little conceptual distinction between the resulting productivity indexes and existing financial ratios (e.g., return on investment).

The third is the so-called Farrell approach, which was devised by Farrell (1957) and further advanced by agricultural economists such as Bressler (1966), Seitz (1970), Boles (1971), and others. The Farrell approach utilizes the production function as its measurement base and estimates the *relative* level of a firm's technical efficiency by where it is positioned within the production "frontier." This approach enables firms to assess their relative efficiencies vis-à-vis other firms in the industry. It also allows firms operating multiple establishments (e.g., plants, stores, etc.) to make interfirm comparisons. The approach, however, has not been widely accepted, primarily because of the complexities involved in the estimation process.

The fourth is the "industrial engineering" approach towards productivity measurement postulated recently by Greenberg (1973) and the Bureau of Labor Statistics (1977). This approach differs from other measurement approaches in its use of time study data to derive a measure of output. Greenberg, for example, derives output of a manufacturing firm by multiplying the physical units of different products manufactured with "the number of manhours required to make each product at a certain time period" (Greenberg, 1973, p. 19). This approach is labeled the industrial engineering approach since industrial engineers have long been associated with developing man-hour requirement data through use of various time-study techniques. Among other things, proponents of this approach argue that the output measure expressed in man-hours, or time, is preferred to those output measures expressed in monetary units (e.g., sales, gross margin, etc.) since the former is not affected by price changes over time. This advantage becomes especially important when inflation reaches a high rate and adjustments are needed to eliminate the upward bias on output because of price increases. One of the major drawbacks of this approach, however, lies in the fact that man-hour requirement data need to be constructed "from scratch," a step necessitating a painstaking data-gathering process.

The fifth is the "surrogate" approach found most often in the organization literature. Researchers have often used such measures as absenteeism and employee turnover as surrogates for productivity of a plant or a group of workers. Some have constructed an index of employee satisfaction and equated it with productivity. Although these attempts in the field of organization add a *human* dimension to productivity research, they do little to advance the measurement task at the micro level. Most of the surrogate measures relate more directly to the quality of the labor input.

The preferred measure of productivity may depend, to a large extent, on the uses that managers have in mind:

- If, as in the case of Eli Lilly and Alcoa, management is interested in comparing the corporate performance with that of the industry, the measure of productivity needs to correspond to the total factor productivity index computed by the Bureau of Labor Statistics;
- If management's primary interest is in determining the results produced by recently acquired equipment or machinery (i.e., capital), a partial index of capital productivity may be more relevant;
- If management of a labor-intensive operation is interested in comparing productivity levels across its multiple establishments at one point in time, a dollar-based measure such as sales per man-hour may suffice (provided the selling prices do not vary across establishments and the product mix remains constant);
- But if management wants to track productivity growth rates over time, the measures to be used have to be properly adjusted for inflation rates;
- If management is considering building productivity improvement into an employee incentive program, an accurate and equitable measure of labor productivity is necessary; use of labor weights appears appropriate in such a case.

Firms are free to develop as many measures of productivity as they see fit. But since user needs differ from situation to situation, there could be as many measures of productivity as there are situations. Firms also should realize that some measures of productivity are better than others. As discussed in the next section, a preferred index of productivity must be a valid measure in addition to being a useful measure.

4.2. RECONCEPTUALIZING PRODUCTIVITY

The concern for validity raises the question of whether the productivity index genuinely measures what should be measured. This question brings the discussion back to the drawing board in defining what productivity is and what it is not. Most experts agree on the basic definition of productivity—that it is a measure of the efficiency with which output is generated from resources or inputs expended. Most of them also agree that productivity should be made operational as a ratio of output to input. Output traditionally has been most readily identified with the flow of products from factories. Under this prevailing view, output is represented by the quantity of tangible goods produced by the firm or plant over some specified period of time. This section of the paper will argue that such a view is not a valid conceptualization of output for purposes of this paper. On the input side, this paper will assume two available formulations of input (i.e., partial input and total factor input) and devote little attention to its discussion.

Under the prevailing view of output, Bucklin (1978, p. 20) notes that "measurement is accomplished by counting the units—so many television sets or jars of jam. The resultant quantity is readily understandable." Or if different goods are produced within a plant, such a view holds that output of the plant can be represented by adding the number of goods together, using dollar values as common denominators. The emphasis is still on tangible products.

A production-oriented concept of output poses several problems, even for a manufacturer. Take a manufacturer of a television set as an example. What comes out of the factory may be a tangible product, but certain services are added to the factory output in the form of packaging, warranty, customer instructions, financing, delivery arrangements, and so forth. These services are additional values *embodied* in the product. A computer manufacturer provides another example of the importance of embodied services. Besides offering the hardware itself, a computer manufacturer provides "peripheral" services in the form of application aids, programming services, training programs, and repair and maintenance. To say that a manufacturer's output consists solely of tangible products is, therefore, too simplistic. It includes both tangible goods produced in the factory and the services embodied in them.

The service embodiment concept applies as much to a food retailer as it does to a manufacturer. Although what are on sale are tangible items (i.e., food, health and beauty aids, and general merchandise items), food retailers add to the salability of these items by providing unit pricing information (i.e., price per pound) on shelf labels, marking the last date by which some perishable items must be sold (known as open dating), cutting up and wrapping meat in smaller portions, or trimming less-than-fresh sections off fresh produce items. Value is thus added to items carried by food retailers through these and other services embodied in them.

Does this analogy mean that a food retailer's output can also be conceptualized as consisting of both tangible products and embodied services? Not necessarily. For a vertically integrated food retailer, Company A, such a conceptualization applies to a limited number of private-label items manufactured in its own plants. Suppose that Company A produces its own instant coffee. The output that Company A generates would consist of (1) the tangible product; (2) services embodied into the product at the manufacturing level in the form of nutritional labeling, packaging, brand name, and usage directions; and (3) additional services embodied in the product at the store or retail level.

But for a majority of other products, which Company A buys directly from the manufacturers, *total* output consists of the sum of (1) the manufacturers' output defined as tangible products and embodied services that Company A purchases from them, and (2) embodied services added to these products at the store or retail level. The latter category of output is services generated from its internal resources while the former is work that has been previously accomplished by external sources (i.e., manufacturers). Therefore, for products purchased from manufacturers, *real* output generated by Company A consists only of (2), or services. So, for Company A, *real* output (or output generated by the company's internal employment of capital, labor, materials, and other resources) consists of both tangible products and embodied services only in the case of private-label goods that it manufactures. For the rest of the goods purchased from outside, *real* output consists only of services embodied at the retail level.

Similarly, *real* output for Company B, a food retailer that does not have manufacturing facilities, is limited to services that it adds to products and services purchased from outside.[4] *Total* output, on the other hand, corresponds to all the work that has been accomplished by members of the marketing system (i.e., suppliers, manufacturers, wholesalers, retailers, service organizations, and others) into making the goods and services salable to the consumer.[5]

The discussion thus far has focused on the meaning of output from the point of view of the manufacturer and the retailer, but not from the consumer's point of view. The question to be raised here is whether or not a valid definition of output should reflect the consumer's perspective.

Past research in consumer behavior has shown that the consumer may be buying much more than just the "physical thing" and the services embodied in it. In Levitt's (1969) words, "People don't buy the product; they buy the expectations of benefits." These expectations, as the following example shows, go beyond what goes into making a product (Levitt, 1980, p. 84):

> An automobile is not simply a machine for movement visibly or measurably differentiated by design, size, color, options, horsepower, or miles per gallon. It is also a complex symbol denoting status, taste, rank, achievement, aspiration, and (these days) being "smart"—that is, buying fuel economy rather than display.

A product, then, represents a bundle of attributes that separately provide utiiities or value to the consumer. For some products, such as a car, symbolic attributes play a far more important role than product attributes.

A necessary condition for the consumer perspective to be incorporated into the output concept, however, is that accurate measures of all consumer utilities be made available. Despite recent methodological advancements in measuring consumer utilities (e.g., conjoint measurement), consumer research has not reached the stage of development where these attitudinal measures could be used reliably to indicate company performance. At the present time, practical disadvantages stemming from possible measurement errors outweigh any conceptual advantages of expanding the meaning of output beyond "goods and services."

In summary, this section has pointed out that a valid concept of output should go beyond the prevailing view of output as the "physical thing" to include embodied services. But at the present time, it cannot go to the other extreme of being viewed as a "symbol" or "benefit expectation." Distinction has been made between *total* and *real* output. If the objective is to isolate the unduplicated output generated by one member of the marketing system (as is the case in this paper), then the *real* output measure is preferred. The task that lies ahead consists of making *real* output operational at the retail level.

4.3. MEASURING OUTPUT

The measurement approach best suited to make the new concept of output operational is the industrial engineering (IE) approach. As described earlier, this approach enables output to be calculated using "man-hour requirement" (commonly known as standard time) as the weighting factor. This weight represents the expected amount of man-hours required by store employees to "process" or "service" a product. As such, they are ideally suited to expressing output as the amount of service provided.

These weights are also useful in measuring the amount of output generated only at the retail level (i.e., *real* output). Only work conducted within the store is included in these weights. Work accomplished outside of the store (by manufacturers or wholesalers) is excluded. In contrast, take the selling prices of the products that are commonly used as weights. These weights include what the retailer paid for goods and services to outside organizations, as well as the services added internally by the retailer. Use of selling prices as weights, therefore, will lead to a construction of a *total* output measure.

But the task of constructing a data base of these preferred weights is not easy. It requires the development of a completely new and custom-made data base by using a time and motion technique known as work sampling (otherwise known as a ratio-delay study). Compared to other time and motion techniques (such as stopwatch or micro-motion studies), work sampling is well suited for situations where a large number of products, employees, and job functions are involved and where these functions are nonroutine in nature. Such situations exist within the food retail chain for which the study was conducted.

A retail food chain provided an excellent unit of analysis for several reasons. First of all, as indicated earlier, the food-retailing industry has been plagued by declining productivity growth rates in recent years. Firms within the industry, therefore, are very receptive towards efforts directed at measuring productivity more accurately. Second, most of the firms are currently employing some measure of productivity such as "sales per man-hour" or "payroll as a percentage of sales." As a result, the new measure can be tested against existing measures to ascertain its validity. Third, a large part of the work that is conducted within a retail food store is nonroutine and customer oriented. Hence the methodology developed here will be applicable to businesses or institutions with similar work characteristics. Many organizations within the service sector could benefit from this study. To the extent that the service sector accounts for more than half of the gross domestic product and the employment of the United States (Eiglier and Langeard, 1977), this contribution is not an insignificant one.

The data development process for a man-hour–weighted measure of output (hereafter referred to as TIME) proceeds in three phases: premeasurement tasks, development of a time standard, and construction of TIME. Each phase is described in further detail in the following sections.

4.3.1. Premeasurement Phase

In order for work sampling to function properly, three preliminary tasks need to be completed. They consist of (1) specifying all the elements of work that take place within the store, (2) grouping over eight thousand items carried in the store into a manageable number of product categories, and (3) estimating the number of total observations required to assure representativeness.

A method study was conducted to carry out the first task, specifying the elements of work.[6] Close to one hundred distinct elements of work were delineated. They included (1) product-oriented functions such as opening boxes, stocking, pricing, and wrapping; (2) customer-oriented functions such as carrying customers' bags and cashing checks; and (3) administrative functions such as ordering and record keeping.

The second task consisted of grouping all the items within the store into approximately one hundred discernible product categories. One of the most important criteria for grouping items into specific product categories was the physical make-up of the product, which to a large extent was found to determine the amount of processing or servicing time required.

The third task, estimating the total number of observations needed to obtain a reliable sample of recordings, was determined through use of some statistical assumptions. Assuming that an observation of a work element is a Bernoulli trial (and therefore distributed binomially) and that the normal distribution is a satisfactory approximation of the binomial distribution for a large sample size, standard deviation can be calculated by:

$$\sigma_p = \sqrt{\frac{p\,(1-p)}{N}}, \tag{4.1}$$

where σ_p is the standard deviation of the sample, p is the percentage of the work element being sought, and N is the total number of random observations required. By designating $p = 0.10$, the confidence interval to be 95 percent (i.e., approximately two sigma), and $2\sigma_p = .005$, N was computed to equal 14,400.[7]

4.3.2. Development of Standard Time

With the preliminary task completed, standard time can now be computed for each of the approximately one hundred product categories. The computation proceeds in three steps. The following illustrates how data were collected in one store.

The first step involves a meticulous recording of the specific work performed by the store employees and their pace of work during the study period. Recording is accomplished by a group of experienced engineers who make several rounds of observations per day with electronic scanning cards in their hands. One such card records the activity of one employee at a given time. So, if there are twenty employees in the store at the time of the observation, an engineer fills out twenty cards in one round. It usually takes two weeks to record 14,400 cards or observations. Each card would contain, among other things, information on the product category being serviced, the work element being performed for that product category, and the pace rating of the employee at a given point in time.

The work sampling technique produces the following three sets of data that later become an integral part of the standard time measure:

O = total number of observations,
N_{wp} = number of observations of work element w associated with product category p,
R_{wp} = pace rating of store employee when conducting work element w associated with product category p.

In addition, two sets of store data are collected to calculate standard time. One is the man-hour data (H), and the other is product movement data (M_p):

H = total number of man-hours actually clocked for all store personnel (includes all hours except lunch breaks),
M_p = total movement of product category p (beginning and ending inventory taken into account).

Given these data, the second step is to calculate what is known in industrial engineering as normal time.[8] It is equivalent to standard time less allowances for rest and personal allowances. It is represented as

$$T_p = \sum_{w=1}^{e} \left(\frac{N_{wp} \cdot H \cdot \bar{R}_{wp}}{M_p \cdot O} \right), \tag{4.2}$$

where T_p is equal to normal time for product category p, $\bar{R}_{wp}$ is average pace rating calculated by dividing R_{wp} into N_{wp}, and e is the total number of work elements.

To clarify equation (4.2), consider the following example: Assume only four work elements are associated with one product category. H and O are assumed to be 2,400 hours and 14,400 observations, respectively. Dividing H into O (i.e., 2,400/14,400 = 0.1667) gives K, which is the constant time weight of each observation. Also assume that $\bar{R}_{wp}$ and N_{wp} are as shown below and that M_p = 10,000 lb. Then, normal time is calculated as shown in Table 4.1 and equation (4.2*a*) as follows:

Table 4.1. Simplified Calculation of Normal Time for Product Category

Work Element w	*Average Pace Rating*		*No. of Observations*		*Constant Time Weight*		*Man-hour Requirement for* w
	$(\bar{R}_{wp})$	×	(N_{wp})	×	(K)	=	(MH_{wp})
Open box	1.00		50		.1667		8.34
Stock	0.98		100		.1667		16.34
Face display	1.02		150		.1667		25.51
Change price	0.96		60		.1667		9.62
Total							59.81

$$T_p = \frac{\sum_{w=1}^{4} MH_{wp}}{M_p} = \frac{59.81}{10{,}000} = .5981 \text{ man-hours per 100 lb.} \tag{4.2a}$$

The third step converts normal time into standard time by adjusting for rest and personal time (A) using the following formula:

$$S_p = T_p\left(\frac{1}{1 - A}\right), \tag{4.3}$$

where S_p is the standard time for product category p. A separate time study conducted by the retail food chain found the percentage of actual working time allocated to rest and personal allowance to be 7.15 percent (i.e., A = .0715). Continuing the previous example, S_p then becomes

$$S_p = \left(\frac{0.5981 \text{ man-hours}}{100 \text{ lb.}}\right)(1.077)$$

$$= \frac{0.6441 \text{ man-hours}}{100 \text{ lb.}}.$$

4.3.3. Development of TIME

The final phase of the data development process involves the creation of a time-weighted output measure (TIME), derived by multiplying the product movement data with standard times. This process can be better understood using a simplified illustration using synthetic data. For a store carrying only six product categories, for example, TIME (i.e., $TIME_p$ summed over p) is calculated as shown in Table 4.2.

Several clarifications are in order before examining the arithmetic. First of all, notice that the movement data and their corresponding standard times are expressed in units for grocery items and in pounds for meat and produce items. The distinction is necessary because standardized units cannot be assigned to most meat and produce items. For example, tomatoes are sold either in loosely displayed form or in prepackaged form. Meats, on the other hand, are mostly prepackaged but vary considerably in size. Actual product movement of these products in most cases is more accurately measured on the basis of pounds.

Secondly, notice that the synthetic standard times assigned to each item on Table 4.2 intuitively correspond to the amount of time required to "process" that item. Meat and produce items, in general, require more attention by store employees because of their perishability and consequently have higher standard times assigned than grocery items. Within the grocery department, milk has a higher standard time than cereal because more employee attention is directed at milk to keep it from spoiling and to maintain the open-dating system. Even within a same product category, such as tomatoes, prepackaged tomatoes could have a higher standard time than loosely displayed tomatoes by virtue of the fact that store employees have

Table 4.2. Simplified Computation of Output Weighted by Standard Time (TIME)

	Store X, XX Weeks Ending XXXX		
Product Categories	*Movement (units: 100)*	*Standard Times (Man-hours per 100 movement)*	*Output (TIME) (Man-hours)*
Grocery			
cereal	2 units	0.4 per 100 units	0.8
milk	4 units	0.6 per 100 units	2.4
Meat			
ground beef	2 lb.	1.0 per 100 lb.	2.0
steak	2 lb.	0.8 per 100 lb.	1.6
Produce			
apple	4 lb.	0.9 per 100 lb.	3.6
lettuce	2 lb.	1.3 per 100 lb.	2.6
Total			13.0

already preselected, preweighed, wrapped, and priced them. These examples illustrate the point that standard time seems to vary directly with the amount of services embodied in the product.

As shown in Table 4.2, TIME for the hypothetical store totals 13.0 man-hours. It is computed by multiplying the product movement data by the respective standard times and summing across six product categories. In reality, TIME would be substantially higher since summation would be across 100 product categories instead of six.

Thus far, the new measure of output was developed based on data from only one store. Work sampling studies, however, were conducted in twenty-five stores, each store producing slightly different standard times for each of the 100 or so product categories.[9] Since one of the key reasons for establishing standard times was to set a company-wide norm that applied to all 180 stores, an "average" or "constant" standard time was calculated for each product category.[10] "Average" standard time for a product category was calculated by (1) plotting the total man-hour requirement data (i.e., MH_{wp} in Table 4.1 or the numerator in equation [2*a*]) against the movement data (i.e., M_p or the denominator in equation [2*a*]), (2) passing a line of best fit through the twenty-five data points,[11] and (3) setting the slope of that line equal to the "average" or "constant" standard time for the entire chain.[12] The output of each store (TIME) was calculated by multiplying "average" standard time (i.e., $\bar{S}_p$) with the movement data for each product category p and summing across p.

To summarize, this section has outlined the measurement process required to make the *real* concept of output operational for a retail store. TIME, which signifies the expected amount of time needed to service or process the products, has been derived using standard times as weights. The next task is to test whether TIME measures what it purports to measure.

4.4. TESTING THE VALIDITY OF "TIME"

TIME was actually computed for a sample of 180 stores within the chain. By utilizing this data base, this section statistically tests whether or not TIME is a valid measure of output. Two tests of validity are conducted—one to test concurrent validity and the other to test construct validity. A concurrent validity test, as the name implies, is concerned with whether the new indicator "concurs" with other indicators of output. A construct validity test, on the other hand, is concerned with the question of what the indicator is in fact measuring.

Concurrent validity is determined by examining the correlation between TIME and other conventional measures of output. Conventional measures included in this study are dollar volume of sales (SALE), gross margin-weighted output (GM), total number of pounds sold (LB), and total number of units sold (UNIT). If the correlation is high and in the predicted direction, TIME is said to have concurrent validity. The Pearson correlation coefficients (on a cross-sectional sample of 180 stores) between TIME and SALE, GM, LB, and UNIT taken one at a time are all above 0.99 ($p \leq .001$ level) and are in the right direction.[13] This simple test confirms the less important of the two validity tests.

The more important concern is whether or not TIME actually measures what it is supposed to measure, i.e., services provided to consumers. Services to consumers at retail stores are hypothesized to be better represented in TIME than in SALE and GM. Although standard time (the weighting factor for TIME) incorporates product-embodied services directly into measuring output, selling prices (the weighting factor for SALE) and gross margin dollars (the weighting factor for GM) only weakly represent services at the retail level. Both selling prices and gross margin dollars incorporate a multitude of factors (such as changes in supply and demand, economies realized in purchasing, degree of price discounting, or competitive pressures) that have little relationship to consumer services provided at the retail level.

If the above argument were true, then one would expect the ratio of SALE/TIME and GM/TIME to have a negative relationship to consumer services offered at the retail level (SERV). That is to say, since the two numerators are expected to reflect services less than the denominator, the ratios are expected to be inversely correlated to SERV. SERV is indicated as a ratio of direct consumer services offered at the front end to total front-end hours. These services, which are expressed in man-hours, include (1) cashing checks, handling money orders, renting equipment, and accepting food stamps; and (2) attending customers with infants and children, offering extra express checkout stands, offering additional carry-out services, and so forth. The first set of services was measured through work sampling while the second was assigned fixed man-hours on the basis of store surveys and interviews.

The correlation coefficients are -0.49 between SALE/TIME and SERV and -0.50 between GM/TIME and SERV. The coefficients are significant at the $p \leq .001$ level and are in the predicted direction, thereby confirming the hypothesis that services are better represented in the new measure of output than in existing conventional measures.

4.5. PRODUCTIVITY INDEXES

Two productivity indexes are constructed based on the new measure of output. One is labor productivity and the other is total factor productivity. This section of the paper briefly describes what measures of input were utilized to construct these two indexes.

Labor productivity (LP) is made operational as a ratio of TIME to actual man-hours worked. Working hours of all store employees—including managers, administrative clerks, and part-timers—are aggregated. Both the numerator and the denominator, then, are expressed in man-hour units.

Total factor productivity (TFP) is made operational as a ratio of TIME to a measure of three input factors—labor, capital, and land. These input factors, however, are expressed either in dollar units or in "converted" man-hour units. To express input in dollar units, the three input factors are indicated as follows:

Labor: Deflated salary for hours actually worked (i.e., salary less paid vacation, holiday, and sick leave);

Capital: Depreciation on all machineries, equipments, and fixtures deflated by the wholesale price index of electrical equipment provided in the *Monthly Labor Review;*

Land: Lease expenses for building and land deflated by a price index of building costs published by the U.S. Department of Commerce in the *Census of Construction.*

To express input in "converted" man-hour units, the dollar measures of capital and land are converted to equivalent man-hours and added to actual man-hours worked. Equivalent man-hours are estimated by dividing the dollar values of capital and land by the hourly wage rate, as shown by Kendrick and Creamer (1965).

Several statistical tests were run to evaluate the validity of the LP index and the two TFP indexes (for more details, see Takeuchi, 1977, pp. 245–300). Concurrent validity was tested using correlation analysis, and construct validity was tested using multiple regression analysis. Validity of the LP index is strongly supported in these tests. But, not surprisingly, validity of the two TFP indexes is not as strongly supported by these tests. The two TFP indexes were nested with measurement problems associated with making capital and land operational (see Takeuchi, 1977, pp. 291–300). Further developmental work is essential before TFP measures can be made useful to management.

4.6. CONCLUSION

The objective of this paper has been to develop a measure of productivity that managers can put to effective use. One of the major obstacles towards achieving this objective was seen as the inadequacy of current measures of output in representing the entire domain of what output should encompass. Output was reconceptualized to reflect the importance of services and was made operational using an engineering approach. The end result was a standard time-weighted measure of output, which was used as the numerator for two productivity indexes.

It is hoped that the results of this paper will serve two useful purposes. First of all, it is hoped that managers engaged in labor-intensive operations (i.e., administrative work, white-collar jobs, government, service, and so forth) will be able to apply the basic measurement approach presented in this paper. Because the IE approach makes measurement of services possible, it is suited to work in many nonproduction-oriented operations. Second, managers should be warned against the careless use of convenient data as surrogate measures of productivity. Before managers are able to analyze such interesting questions as the following:

Is government intervention hurting productivity?
Why are some establishments more productive than others?
Do incentive plans help to increase productivity?
Does organizing employees into work groups help to improve productivity?
Is productivity increasing as fast as inflation or wage rates?

they need to invest time in constructing a useful, valid, and sometimes custom-made data base from which productivity measures can be derived. If productivity is conceptualized, or measured incorrectly, or both, then the results of the analyses in terms of interesting questions like the above become meaningless.

Whether productivity research at the micro level will reach the sophistication currently achieved at the macro level is contingent upon the development of good measures of productivity and their diffusion into as many organizations as possible. Why be so concerned about micro-level productivity? Because the whole (macro) is equal to the sum of its parts (micro).

NOTES

1. See the following sources on this topic: Balk (1978); Hayward (1976); Melman (1971); Fuchs (1969); Bernstein (1977).

2. For a descriptive summary of divergent views of the causes of productivity slowdown, see McConnell (1979).

3. Both *total factor* productivity and *labor* productivity indexes have been developed through the macro-oriented approach.

4. *Real* output, as used in this paper, is similar in content to the more familiar concept of *value added.* At the retail level, both concepts specify the extra value or services that the retailer adds to goods purchased from outside so that they may be better accepted by consumers.

5. *Total* output, then, can be approximated by final dollar sales to consumers. In a sense, it is the sum of all the value added provided by members of the marketing system.

6. A *method study,* also known as motion study in industrial engineering, is a scientific technique designed to observe, record, and critically examine an existing or proposed way of conducting work. Recording often involves the use of charts, diagrams, or motion pictures. A more efficient method of operation is often developed as a result of a method study.

7. For a 95 percent confidence interval, equation (4.1) can be rewritten as

$$2\sigma_p = 2\sqrt{\frac{p\,(1-p)}{N}} = .005.$$

Substituting in the values of $p = 0.1$, N is computed to equal 14,400. This means that if a work element is performed 10 percent of the time, you need to take 14,400 samples so that you will have a 95 percent chance of having your estimated p fall in the interval between .095 and .105.

8. *Normal time* is defined as "the time required for the standard operator to perform the operation when working at a standard pace without delay for personal reasons or unavoidable circumstances" according to Niebel (1976, p. 679).

9. The variation in the standard time among the stores was surprisingly small. This result probably reflects the company's attempt to standardize the size and layout of the store and operating procedures within the store.

10. By having the same standard times for all the stores, the company sets a norm on how many hours the store would be *expected* to spend on, say, dog food. If, for example, store A sells the same amount of dog food as store B, but store A spends less *actual* man-hours "processing" it, then store A would be a more labor productive store than B.

11. The lines were drawn manually with most of the lines passing through the origin. Lines that did not pass through the origin were mostly for meat and produce product categories that required some setup time. A preferred way of estimating the slope is through regression analysis.

12. Alternatively, the company could have taken (1) a simple average of the standard times or (2) the standard time of the best store. Plotting has the advantage of being able to spot outliers in the data more readily than simple averages and to reflect economies of scale more readily than simple averages. Selecting the standard times of the best store (i.e., the lowest time values) would be effective in bringing the laggards up to par, but may result in these stores cutting unnecessary corners too rapidly or in the entire productivity measurement project's being perceived as an inequitable system.

13. $p \leq .001$ means that there is a 99.9 percent chance or better of the coefficient being different from zero.

REFERENCES

Balk, Walter L., ed., 1978, "Productivity in Government: A Symposium," *Public Administration Review,* January–February:1–50.

Bernstein, Peter L., 1977, "Productivity: Rewards Needed for Taking Risks," *New York Times,* April 24, p. F4.

Boles, James N., 1971, *The 1130 Farrell Efficiency System—Multiple Products, Multiple Factors,* Berkeley: University of California, Giannini Foundation of Agricultural Economics.

Bressler, R. G., 1966, "The Measurement of Productive Efficiency," *Western Farm Economics Association, Proceedings.*

Bucklin, Louis P., 1978, *Productivity in Marketing,* Chicago: American Marketing Association.

Cocks, Douglas L., 1974, "The Measurement of Total Factor Productivity for a Large U.S. Manufacturing Corporation," *Business Economics,* September:7–20.

Craig, Charles E., and Clark Harris, 1973, "Total Productivity Measurement at the Firm Level," *Sloan Management Review,* Spring:13–29.

Daly, Keith, and Arthur Neef, 1978, "Productivity and Unit Labor Costs in 11 Industrialized Countries, 1977," *Monthly Labor Review,* November:11–17.

Davis, Hiram S., 1955, *Productivity Accounting,* Philadelphia: University of Pennsylvania Press.

Eiglier, Pierre, and Eric Langeard, 1977, "A New Approach to Service Marketing," in Pierre Eiglier et al. (1977).

Eiglier, Pierre, et al., 1977, *Marketing Consumer Services: New Insights,* Cambridge, Mass.: Marketing Science Institute.

Farrell, M. J., 1957, "The Management of Productive Efficiency," *Journal of the Royal Statistical Society,* Series A, 120, Pt. 3:253–90.

Flint, Jerry, 1979, "Lagging Productivity: Planners Are Stymied," *New York Times,* January 27, p. 26.

Fuchs, Victor R., 1969, *The Service Economy,* New York: National Bureau of Economic Research.

Gantz, Marvin E., Jr., 1976, "Productivity Measurement in Alcoa," in National Center for Productivity and Quality of Working Life (1976).

Gold, Bela, 1955, *Foundations of Productivity Analysis: Guides to Economic Theory and Managerial Control,* Pittsburgh: University of Pittsburgh Press.

Greenberg, Leon, 1973, *A Practical Guide to Productivity Measurement,* Washington, D.C.: Bureau of National Affairs.

Hayward, Nancy S., 1976, "The Productivity Challenge," *Public Administration Review,* September–October:544–50.

Herman, Arthur, 1978, "Productivity Increased during 1977 in a Majority of Selected Industries," *Monthly Labor Review,* September:54–56.

Kendrick, John, and Daniel Creamer, 1965, *Measuring Company Productivity,* Studies in Business Economics, no. 89, New York: National Industrial Conference Board.

Levitt, Theodore, 1969, *The Marketing Mode,* New York: McGraw-Hill.

———, 1976, "The Industrialization of Service," *Harvard Business Review,* September–October:63–74.

———, 1980, "Marketing Success through Differentiation—of Anything," *Harvard Business Review,* January–February:83–91.

Martin, Harold W., 1964, "Productivity Costing and Control," *Productivity Measurement Review,* May:12–59.

McConnell, Campbell R., 1979, "Why Is U.S. Productivity Slowing Down?" *Harvard Business Review,* March–April:36–61.

Melman, Seymour, 1971, *The War Economy of the United States,* New York: St. Martin's Press.

National Center for Productivity and Quality of Working Life, 1976, *Improving Productivity through Industry and Company Measurement,* Series 2, Washington, D.C.: Gov't. Printing Office (October).

New York Stock Exchange, 1979, *Reaching a Higher Standard of Living,* New York: New York Stock Exchange, January.

Niebel, Benjamin, 1976, *Motion and Time Study,* Homewood, Ill.: Richard D. Irwin.

Seitz, Wesley D., 1970, "The Measurement of Efficiency Relative to a Frontier Production Function," *American Journal of Agricultural Economics* 62 (November):505–11.

Takeuchi, Hirotaka, 1977, "Productivity Analysis as a Resource Management Tool in the Retail Trade," unpublished Ph.D. dissertation, University of California, Berkeley.

———, 1978*a*, "Misconceptions of the Productivity Concept: The Genesis of Empirical Problems in Productivity Research," *AIDS Proceedings 1978,* American Institute for Decision Sciences.

———, 1978*b*, "Productivity Analysis as Useful Management Tools," *AIDS Proceedings 1978,* American Institute for Decision Sciences.

Takeuchi, Hirotaka, and Louis P. Bucklin, 1977, "Productivity in Retailing, Retail Structure, and Public Policy," *Journal of Retailing,* Spring.

U.S. Bureau of Labor Statistics, 1977, "Report on Productivity Gains in Selected Industries," *Monthly Labor Review,* January:80–83.

II A RANGE OF STUDIES AT THE MICRO LEVEL

5 A MODELING APPROACH TO PRODUCTIVITY DEALS

George Cosmetatos and Samuel Eilon

Negotiations between employers and employees on pay and working conditions tend to become increasingly protracted and complex. Apart from the goal of reaching an agreement that will satisfy both parties, there is a need to take account of whatever statutory or voluntary policies are currently in vogue regarding incomes and prices. Thus, the negotiators have to consider an increasing number of issues, involving on the one hand pay and working conditions—such as basic and overtime rates, redundancies and severance payment, duration of the working week, holidays, pension schemes, and other benefits—while on the other hand they have to weigh the consequences of these factors on various performance measures such as output, unit cost, and profit levels, which are further affected by pricing policies and promotional activities. These complexities give rise to an increasing number of alternatives that the negotiators have to evaluate, and it therefore appears that the availability of suitable models, sufficiently simple in structure yet encompassing the most pertinent issues that need to be taken into account, would greatly assist in this evaluation process and become a tool both sides could use in their search for a mutually beneficial and/or acceptable solution.

In this paper we present a methodology for structuring models to suit the needs of the negotiators and to incorporate whatever sets of assumptions are appropriate. The models are interrelated and enable their users to assess explicitly and quantitatively the relative effects on partial or aggregate criteria of relative changes in each criterion's constituent elements. Using possible negotiating scenarios as a basis, we also illustrate the conditions under which the benefits to one or both parties are likely to improve or decline, and we highlight some of the conclusions that can be drawn from the analysis.

The employees' objective of seeking an improvement in their living standards is reflected in their demands for higher pay, better working conditions, improved benefits, and security of employment. The degree to which these demands can be fulfilled depends on a variety of factors such as technological change and future prospects in terms of company growth. Over the short term, demand for the firm's product may change due to factors outside the direct control of management (primary change) but also as a result of primary changes in pricing policies, or advertising and promotional activity, or both.

Let

p = unit price for the output,
D = total expenditure on advertising and sales promotion,
V = level of demand measured in physical terms,
p^*, D^*, V_0^* = primary relative changes in p, D, and V (i.e., $p^* = \delta p/p$, etc.).

If we assume that the incremental changes δp, δD, and hence the corresponding relative changes p^*, D^* are expressed in real terms (i.e., that they are adjusted for the effects of inflation), then the primary change in the selling price induces a change in demand, V_1^*, given by

$$V_1^* = -\epsilon p^*, \tag{5.1}$$

where ϵ is the absolute value of the price elasticity of demand (expected to depend on both p and p^*); similarly (see Eilon and Cosmetatos, 1979*a*),

$$V_2^* = \lambda D^*, \tag{5.2}$$

where λ is the "promotion elasticity of demand" (expected to depend on both D and D^*).

The total change in demand, V^*, will be a function of V_0^*, V_1^*, and V_2^*; if we assume that the effects on demand of external factors and those of the relative changes p^*, D^* are independent and additive, then

$$V^* = V_0^* - \epsilon p^* + \lambda D^* \tag{5.3}$$

but it is, of course, possible to modify (5.3) in situations where the independence assumption is thought to be invalid.

Finally, if we assume that there is to be no change in stock level policies, then the total relative change in demand, V^*, needs to be matched by an equal relative change in the level of output. Thus, V^* can be viewed as a primary change imposed on the production department.

5.1. CHANGES IN WORKING HOURS, LABOR PRODUCTIVITY, AND THE SIZE OF THE WORK FORCE

Let

T_b = total hours of normal work per employee in a year,
T_o = total hours of overtime work per employee in a year,
N = average number of employees on the payroll,
$\Pi = V/[(T_b + T_o)N]$, the average labor productivity, assumed here to be the same during both normal and overtime hours of work.

Labor productivity may increase (or, indeed, decrease) for a variety of reasons, such as increased effort, substitution of labor by machines, introduction of technical or managerial innovations, and company policy on recruiting and/or layoffs, to name but a few. This relative change, Π^*, in conjunction with V^*, will affect T_b, and/or T_o, and/or N (see Figure 5.1). Thus, if we assume that T_b, T_o, and N are to change by T_b^*, T_o^*, and N^*, respectively, then we obtain, following the method of incremental analysis (Eilon, 1975), a relationship between Π^*, V^*, T_b^*, T_o^*, and N^*, which can be described by

$$\Pi^* = \frac{V^* - N^* - [(1 - t_o)T_b^* + t_o T_o^*](1 + N^*)}{(1 + N^*)[1 + (1 - t_o)T_b^* + t_o T_o^*]}, \tag{5.4}$$

where $t_o = T_o/(T_b + T_o)$ is the ratio of overtime to total man-hours. As the expression in (5.4) involves relative changes only, it is not difficult to generalize it to the multiproduct case (see, for example, Kurosawa, 1975).

For relatively small N^*, T_b^*, and T_o^*, (5.4) can be simplified to read

$$\Pi^* \simeq V^* - N^* - (1 - t_o)T_b^* - t_o T_o^*. \tag{5.4a}$$

Thus, for example, if the employees place no demands on T_b ($T_b^* = 0$) and the average labor productivity is to remain unchanged, then the relationship between V^*, N^*, and T_o^*, which for $t_o = 0.10$ is depicted in Figure 5.2, highlights the high sensitivity of T_o^* to small changes in V^* or N^*: If, say, the

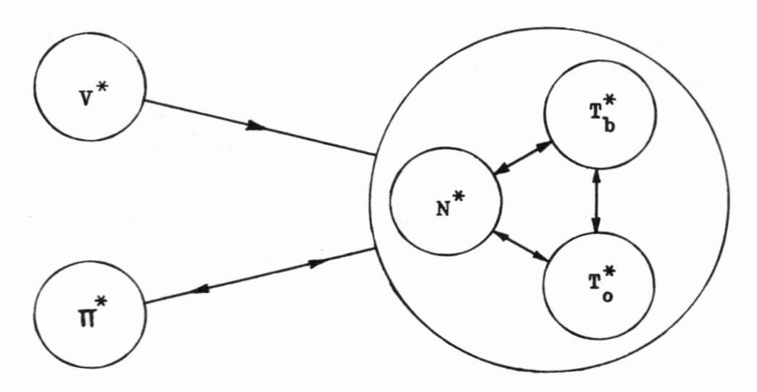

FIGURE 5.1. The Interrelationships between Changes in Labor Productivity, Output, Working Hours, and the Size of the Work Force

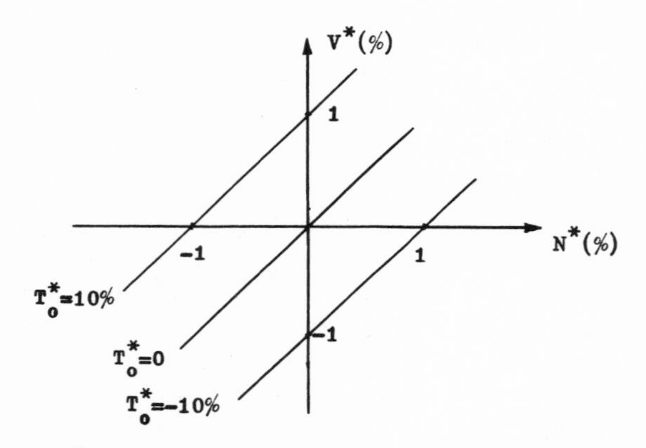

FIGURE 5.2. The Effect on T_o of Small Changes in V, or N ($\Pi^* = T_b^* = 0$), or Both

level of output is expected to fall by 1 percent ($V^* = -0.01$) and yet the employees insist that no layoffs should take place ($N^* = 0$), then the effect on overtime work would be to reduce it by no less than 10 percent. Similarly, if there is to be no change in total volume ($V^* = 0$), then the condition for productivity not to decline ($\Pi^* \geq 0$) becomes, from (5.4*a*),

$$N^* + (1 - t_o)T_b^* + t_o T_o^* \leq 0,$$

and for $t_o = 0.10$ this condition is satisfied to the left of the lines shown in Figure 5.3, so that the trade-off between T_o^* and N^* is clearly depicted for any given level of T_b^*.

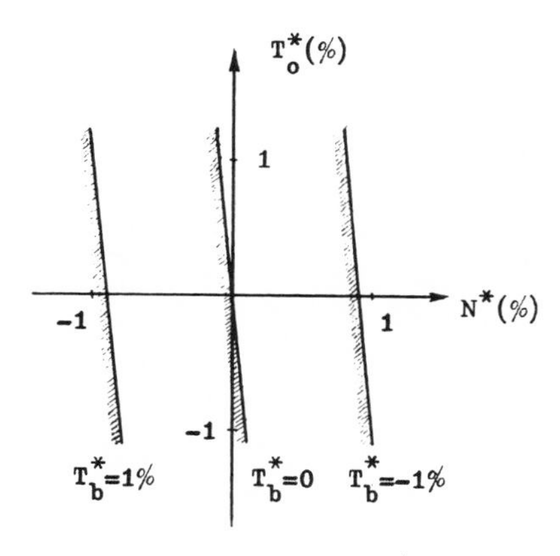

FIGURE 5.3. The Condition $\Pi^* > 0$ ($V^* = 0$)

5.2. CHANGES IN WAGE RATES

Any changes in T_b, T_o, and N have to be considered in conjunction with the employees' demands for wage rate increases in order to determine their effects on the total wage bill.

Let

w_b = average basic rate,
w_h = average holiday rate,
w_o = average overtime rate,
T_h = man-hours of paid holidays per employee in a year,
W = total wage bill in a year.

If we assume that

$$W = W_b + W_h + W_o = w_b T_b N + w_h T_h N + w_o T_o N, \tag{5.5}$$

then it can be shown that the relative changes w_b^*, w_h^*, w_o^*, T_b^*, T_h^*, T_o^*, and N^* (see Figure 5.4) will change the total wage bill by the relative amount

$$W^* = \frac{W_b}{W} W_b^* + \frac{W_h}{W} W_h^* + \frac{W_o}{W} W_o^*, \tag{5.6}$$

where

$$W_j^* = w_j^* + N^*(1 + w_j^*) + (1 + N^*)(1 + w_j^*) T_j^*, \text{ for } j = b, h, o, \tag{5.7}$$

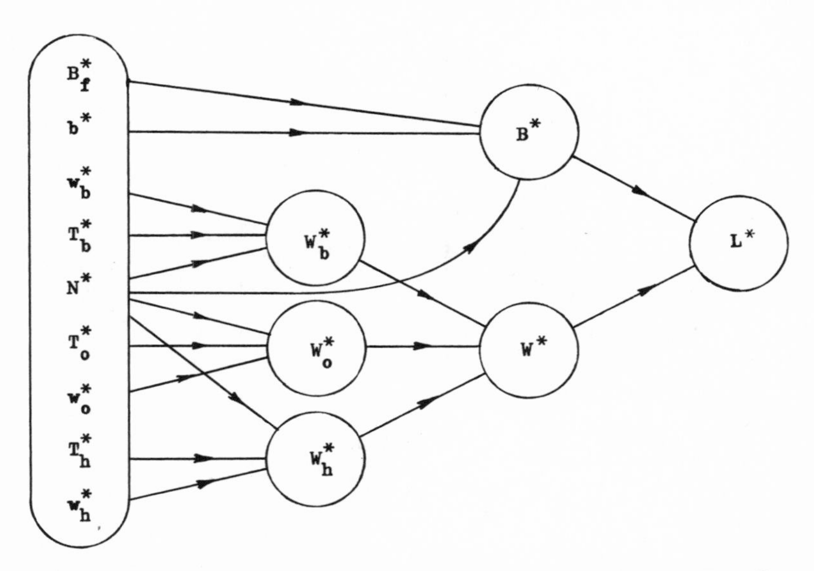

FIGURE 5.4. The Effects of Employees' Demands on Wages, Benefits, and the Total Labor Cost

are, respectively, the relative changes in total basic wage, holiday pay, and overtime pay. For relatively small changes, the expression in (5.7) can be simplified to

$$W_j^* \simeq w_j^* + N^* + T_j^*, \tag{5.7a}$$

so that (5.6) becomes

$$W^* \simeq N^* + \left(\frac{W_b}{W}\right)(w_b^* + T_b^*) + \left(\frac{W_h}{W}\right)(w_h^* + T_h^*) + \left(\frac{W_o}{W}\right)(w_o^* + T_o^*). \tag{5.6a}$$

Alternatively, if W^* is specified, representing, say, an offer being made by the employers to the employees, then it is possible for the employees to use (5.4) and (5.6) or their approximations in order to compare the many feasible solutions that become available.

5.2.1. An Example

Suppose that $T_b^* = T_h^* = 0$, $V^* = 0$, but that the employees put forward demands for an increase in their rates. We have from (5.4*a*)

$$\Pi^* \simeq -N^* - t_o T_o^*, \tag{5.8}$$

and from (5.6*a*), assuming $w_h^* = w_o^* = w_b^*$,

$$W^* \simeq N^* + w_b^* + \left(\frac{W_o}{W}\right) T_o^*. \tag{5.9}$$

Let, also, $t_o = 0.10$ and $W_o/W = 0.14$. Two variations of the problem will now be considered.

$w_b^* = 0.02$ *(in real terms).* Let $\eta = W/N$ denote the total wage per employee. As a result of changes in *W*, or *N*, or both, η will change by

$$\eta^* = \frac{(W^* - N^*)}{(1 + N^*)} \simeq W^* - N^*. \tag{5.10}$$

Figure 5.5 gives a graphical representation of (5.8), (5.9), and (5.10). It can be seen, for example, that

1. If $\Pi^* = 0$ and no change in the size of the labor force takes place (point *A*), then $T_o^* = 0$ and the employees will be better off by 2 percent ($\eta^* = 0.02$);
2. If $N^* = 0$ but Π^* rises by 1.4 percent (point *B*) as a result of, say, improved production methods or technical innovations, then each

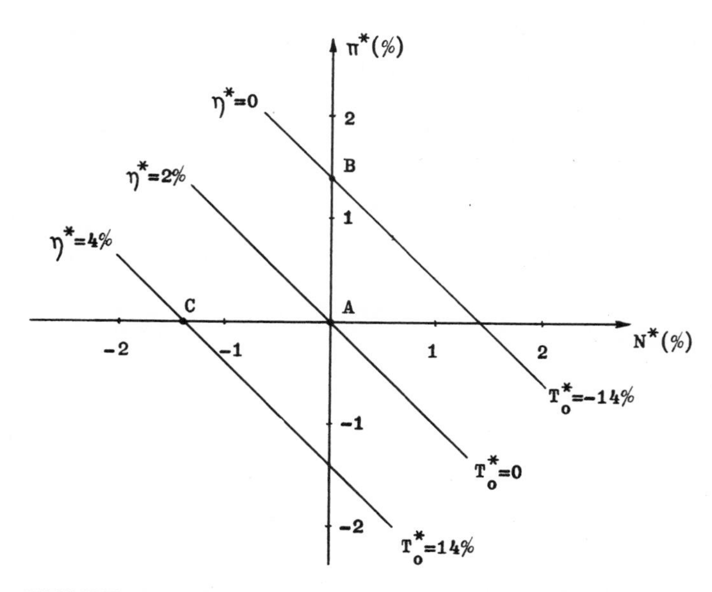

FIGURE 5.5. Effects of a 2 Percent Increase in Rates (example)

employee will enjoy a 2 percent increase in rates but in the end will be no better off in terms of take-home pay ($\eta^* = 0$), because each employee will work 14 percent less overtime;

3. However, if $\Pi^* = 0$ but N falls by 1.4 percent (point C) as a result of, say, natural wastage, then each employee will work 14 percent more overtime and in the end will be 4 percent better off ($\eta^* = 0.04$).

Clearly, the conclusion to draw is that the publicity often given by the media to employees' demands on wage rate increases is ill informed, if not meaningless: Such demands, even if met in full, may bear little relationship to how much better or worse off each employee will become.

$W^* = 0.02$ *(in real terms).* The effect on the total wage per employee of such an offer is derived from formula (5.10): Regardless of how much larger or smaller than 2 percent the wage rate increase turns out to be, each employee will be better off by more than 2 percent only if redundancies take place. As for the effects of $W^* = 0.02$ on w_b, it can be seen from Figure 5.6 that

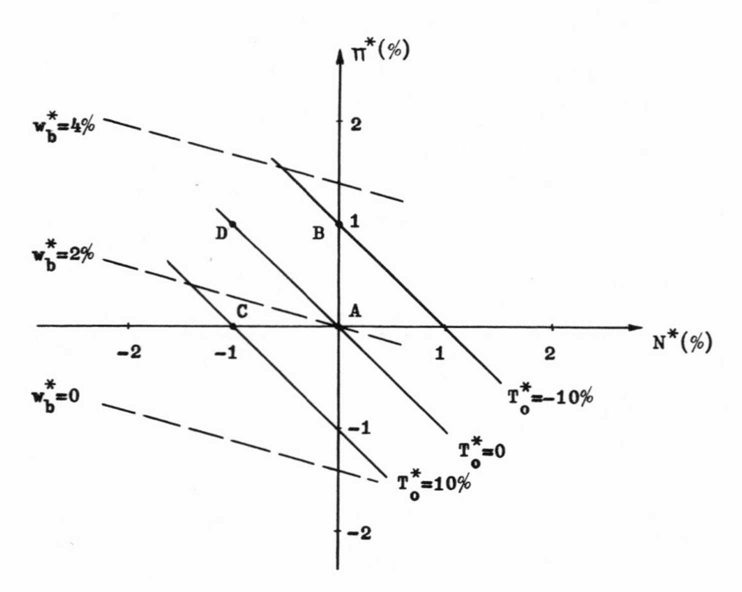

FIGURE 5.6. Effects of a 2 Percent Increase in the Total Wage Bill (example)

1. If $N^* = \Pi^* = 0$ (point A), then $T_o^* = 0$ and $w_b^* = 0.02$;
2. If $N^* = 0$ but Π rises by 1 percent (point B), then $T_o^* = -0.10$ and as a result, the employees will be able to claim an increase of almost 3.5 percent in their rates, although $\eta^* = 0.02$;
3. If $\Pi^* = 0$ but $N^* = -0.01$ (point C), then the resulting wage rate increase will fall short of 2 percent; however, because of increased overtime work ($T_o^* = 0.10$) and the reduction in the size of the work force, each employee who does not become redundant will be better off by 3 percent;
4. If $\Pi^* = 0.01$ and $N^* = -0.01$ (point D), there will be no change in overtime work, as in item 1 above, but the employees on the payroll will be able to enjoy increases higher than 2 percent in both w_b and η.

Thus, depending on the relative importance that the employees attach to η^*, N^*, and T_o^*, and also on the options for changing the average labor productivity that are available, it is possible for the employees' representatives to choose and/or propose to management sets of w_b^*, N^*, and T_o^* values that in their view would best meet the aspirations of their colleagues.

5.3. CHANGES IN BENEFITS

In addition to demanding changes in working hours and wage rates, the employees may place demands on benefits, such as pension schemes, subsidies or discounts, catering facilities, working conditions, and so forth. If it is assumed that the total benefits to employees, B, can be expressed as

$$B = B_f + bN,$$

where B_f denotes benefits independent of N (fixed benefits) and b the variable benefit per employee, then the two primary changes B_f^*, b^* and the relative change N^* in the size of the work force (see Figure 5.4) will change B by

$$B^* = \left(\frac{B_f}{B}\right)B_f^* + \left(\frac{bN}{B}\right)(b^* + N^* + b^*N^*) \simeq \left(\frac{B_f}{B}\right)B_f^* + \left(\frac{bN}{B}\right)(b^* + N^*). \quad (5.11)$$

Finally, the two relative changes W^* and B^*, obtained from (5.6) or (5.6a) and (5.11) will change the total labor cost, $L = W + B$, by

$$L^* = \left(\frac{W}{L}\right)W^* + \left(\frac{B}{L}\right)B^*. \quad (5.12)$$

Thus, the interrelationships quantified in (5.4), (5.6), (5.11), and (5.12), subject to the assumptions made, enable the negotiators to estimate the partial or total effects of a set of demands by the employees, as well as to explore the acceptability or otherwise of the many alternative ways by which a given offer proposed by the employers can be decomposed.

5.4. THE EFFECTS ON THE UNIT COST AND THE PROFIT

The unit cost, *c*, will be affected by the following:

- The change, L^*, in the total "package" consisting of both wages and benefits;
- The change, D^*, in the total expenditure on advertising and sales promotion;
- The change, V^*, in the level of output that will affect the unit fixed cost.

It may be affected by the following:

- The change in the work force size, N^*: If $N^* > 0$, then recruitment or training costs or both may have to be incurred; if $N^* < 0$, then redundancy payments may have to be made;
- The change in the labor productivity, Π^*: It is possible, for example, that an increase in labor productivity can only be achieved by further investment, which will then affect the fixed cost;
- A possible change in the unit variable cost as a result of the change in the level of output (see Cosmetatos, Barbaroussis, and Eilon, 1979, for a more detailed analysis);
- A possible change in the total interest charge caused by a change in the level of borrowings, if the working capital requirements change as a result of the likely change in total costs, or revenue, or both (see Eilon and Cosmetatos, 1977).

For the purpose of simplifying the analysis, we assume in this paper that the effect on the unit cost of the four last factors is negligible. More explicitly, we assume that

- Small changes in the size of the work force can take place at no additional cost; such an assumption is justified if layoffs are possible through natural wastage or if recruitment and training costs are small (for example, when the firm operates a training center whose costs are regarded as fixed);

- Labor productivity can be increased by reducing idle time (through more efficient planning, scheduling, internal communication systems, improved methods, etc.) or inefficient operations (such as unnecessary handling, reprocessing of defective items, and so forth) or both;
- The unit variable cost is not sensitive to small changes in the capacity utilization, or the short-run cost-volume relationship is not known or very difficult to obtain, or both;
- The conditions for the secondary effects on the unit cost of changes in working capital requirements to be small (see Eilon and Cosmetatos, 1979*b*) hold.

Thus, if we set the unit cost c as

$$c = s + \frac{L}{V} + \frac{D}{V} + \frac{F}{V}, \tag{5.13}$$

where s denotes the unit variable cost and F the total fixed cost other than L and D, then the three changes L^*, D^*, and V^* will change the unit cost by

$$c^* = \frac{f_2L^* + f_3D^* - (1 - f_1)V^*}{1 + V^*} \simeq f_2L^* + f_3D^* - (1 - f_1)V^*, \tag{5.14}$$

with f_1, f_2, f_3 representing, respectively, the three cost proportions s/c, $L/(cV)$, $D/(cV)$ in (5.13). It should be noted here that (5.14) does not include the effects of inflation on the unit cost (s^* and F^* have been assumed equal to zero). Therefore, the changes L^* and D^* represent changes in real terms. It is of course possible to relax this implicit assumption, but the expressions (5.1), (5.2), and (5.14) would have to be modified accordingly.

The total profit $Z = (p - c)V$ will then change by (see Eilon and Cosmetatos, 1979*a*)

$$Z^* = V^* + (1/\alpha)(1 + V^*)[p^* - (1 - \alpha)c^*], \tag{5.15}$$

where $\alpha = (p - c)/p$ denotes the profit margin and c^* is obtained from (5.14).

In the special case $p^* = D^* = 0$, the conditions for $c^* < 0$ and $Z^* > 0$ are, respectively,

$$L^* < \frac{(1 - f_1)V^*}{f_2} = L_c^*, \tag{5.16}$$

and for $\alpha > 0$,

$$L^* < L_c^* + \frac{\alpha}{(1 - \alpha)f_2}V^* = L_Z^*. \tag{5.17}$$

The employees, on the other hand, will be better off if

$$\xi^* = \left(\frac{L}{N}\right)^* = \frac{(L^* - N^*)}{(1 + N^*)} \simeq L^* - N^* \tag{5.18}$$

is positive, and the condition for this to happen is, simply,

$$L^* > N^*. \tag{5.19}$$

Thus, if $V^* < 0$, then $L_Z^* < L_c^* < 0$, and none of the three conditions in (5.16), (5.17), and (5.19) can be met if redundancies do not take place. However, in the event that $V^* > 0$, in which case $L_Z^* > L_c^* > 0$ (see Figure 5.7), it is possible for all three conditions to be met even when $N^* > 0$ (pairs of L^*, N^* values within the triangle *ABC*); moreover, if the conditions (5.17) and (5.19) are the only ones to be met, then combinations of L^* and $N^* > 0$ values within the area *BCDE* can also be chosen. The difference $L_Z^* - L_c^*$ measures the relative increase in the total "package" in excess of the one that ensures $c^* < 0$, which could be awarded to the employees, if the total profit is not to decline; and this difference is proportional to V^*, and relatively large if the profit margin is high and the proportion of labor costs to total costs low.

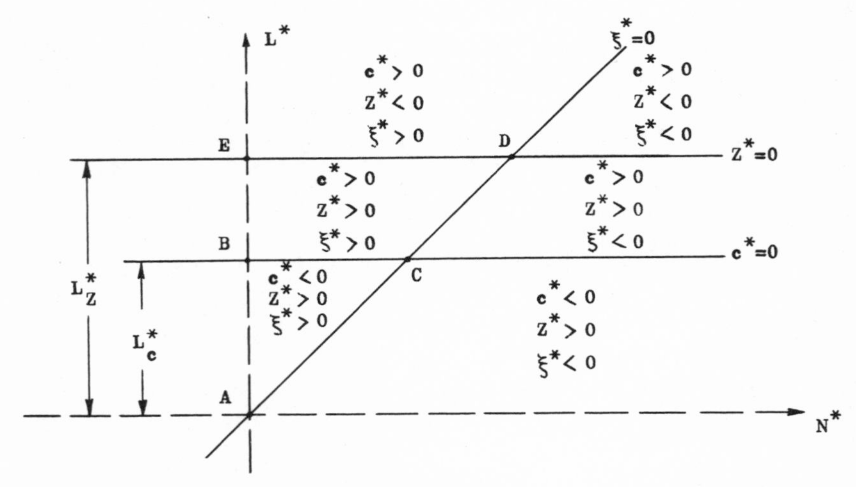

FIGURE 5.7. The Effects of L^*, N^* on c, Z, and ξ

5.5. DEVELOPING MODELS FOR USE IN THE NEGOTIATIONS: AN EXAMPLE

5.5.1. Scenario 1

Change in Demand. If no action to affect the unit price or the total expenditure on advertising and sales promotion is to take place, then the demand for the product is expected to rise by a modest 1 percent ($V^* = V_o^* = 0.01$).

Employees' Demands.

1. $T_b^* = 0$, reflecting no demands put forward by the employees for, say, a shorter working week;
2. $B_f^* = b^* = 0$, reflecting the absence of demands for improved benefits;
3. $w_h^* = w_o^* = w_b^* > 0$, reflecting demands for higher wage rates (in real terms);
4. $T_h^* = 0.10$, reflecting demands for a 10 percent increase in paid holidays;
5. $\xi^* = 0.03$, reflecting demands for a 3 percent increase in the total labor cost per employee (also in real terms).

Employees' Payoffs. The size of the work force should rise in line with the expected rise in output (concessions could be made with regard to this issue provided that N^* remains positive).

Change in the Productivity of Labor. A recent report by the work study group indicates that improvements in materials' handling and production methods can, if implemented, increase output per man-hour by 1.5 percent ($\Pi^* = 0.015$) without requiring additional effort on the employees' part. Management are keen to see these changes introduced but the cooperation of the labor force is deemed essential.

Change in the Unit Cost. It can be assumed that the unit cost will be affected only by the change in the total labor cost and the reduction in the unit fixed cost resulting from the expected increase in the level of output.

Employers' Payoffs. The employers insist that $c^* < 0$ (some concessions could be made provided that Z^* remains positive).

Data.

$t_o = T_o/(T_b + T_o) = 0.10$ — required for the evaluation of (5.4*a*),

$B_f/L = 0.15$
$W/L = 0.75$
$W_h/L = 0.045$
$W_o/L = 0.105$ — required for the evaluation of (5.12) and (5.18),

$f_1 = 0.40$
$f_2 = 0.25$ — required for the evaluation of (5.14) and (5.16),

$\alpha = 0.13$ — required for the evaluation of (5.15) and (5.17).

Evaluation of the Employees' and Employers' Positions.

1. The condition $c^* < 0$ in (5.16) yields $L^* < 0.024$; however, the demand for $\xi^* = 0.03$ put forward by the employees implies, from (5.18), $L^* = 0.03 + N^*$, so that an agreement could become possible only in the event that $N^* < -0.006$;
2. The condition $Z^* > 0$ in (5.17) yields $L^* < 0.030$, so that a compromise offer, say $L^* = 0.027$, would still require layoffs of 0.3 percent despite the 1 percent increase in output;
3. If the employees insist that no reduction in the size of the work force is acceptable and the employers are not prepared to hand over to the employees all the profit increase that would result from the increased sales, then it seems that a possibility worth considering would be to investigate the effectiveness, or otherwise, of trying to stimulate demand further; and this leads to the next scenario.

5.5.2. Scenario 2

Suppose that the marketing department has evidence in support of the view that a 10 percent increase in advertising and promotional expenditure ($D^* = 0.10$) would increase demand by a further 1.2 percent, so that $V^* = V_o^* + V_2^* = 0.01 + 0.012 = 0.022$. Assuming $f_3 = 0.05$, the conditions $c^* < 0$, $Z^* > 0$, derived from (5.14) and (5.15), yield, respectively, $L^* < 0.033$ and $L^* < 0.046$: Along the line segment AB in Figure 5.8, which represents the condition $\xi^* = 0.03$, the employees would clearly favor an agreement close to point *B*, whereas the employers would very much prefer a settlement close to point *A*, which corresponds to lower L^* and N^* and to a larger profit improvement than in the vicinity of *B*.

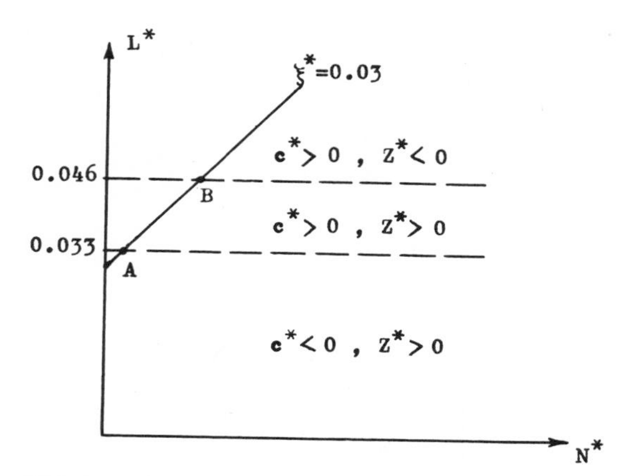

FIGURE 5.8. The Effects on c and Z of L^* and N^* (scenario 2)

5.5.3. Scenario 3

Suppose, finally, that the positive effect on demand of $D^* = 0.10$ is canceled out if at the same time it is decided to increase the unit price by 1 percent. The two conditions $c^* < 0$ and $Z^* > 0$ yield, respectively, $L^* < 0.004$ and $L^* < 0.0564$; it seems therefore that in this case the unit cost is bound to rise if the condition $N^* > 0$ is to be met.

5.5.4. Evaluation of the Alternatives

If the changes leading to higher labor productivity are introduced, then (5.4a) becomes $0.015 = V^* - N^* - 0.1T_o^*$, and the condition $N^* > 0$ is equivalent to $0.1T_o^* < V^* - 0.015$. Thus, subject to $T_o^* < 0.07$ under scenario 2 and $T_o^* < -0.05$ under scenario 3, this condition is met, and the chance that the employees will agree to implement the proposed changes can then be relied on.

Figure 5.9 shows the linear relationships between c^*, Z^*, and N^* for the two cases described under scenarios 2 (solid lines) and 3 (broken lines). It becomes apparent that no scenario is dominant over the other; over the whole range of feasible N^* values the implementation of scenario 3 would lead to higher profit but also to higher unit cost; it seems, therefore, that preference over one or the other depends on the relative importance at-

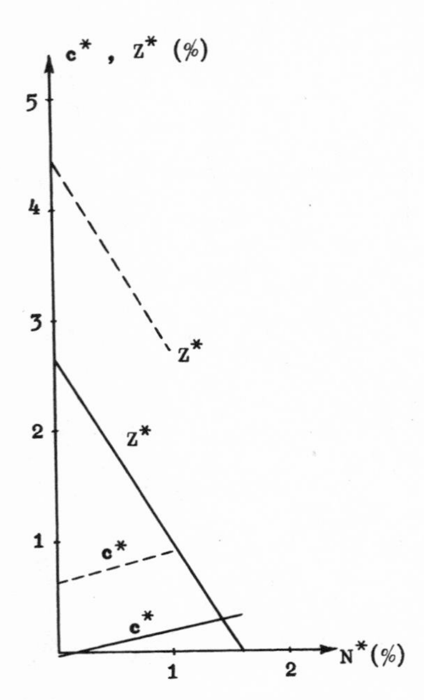

FIGURE 5.9. Relationships between c^*, Z^*, and N^*. (The solid lines refer to scenario 2, and the broken lines to scenario 3.)

tached by management to the two performance measures c^* and Z^*. A second conclusion drawn from Figure 5.9 relates to the degree of conflict between the employees' objectives and the ones of the employers. No "optimal" solution is possible; the solution would still have to be reached on the basis of discussions.

If it is assumed that scenario 3 with $N^* = 0.005$ is agreed upon, leading to $c^* \simeq 0.008$ and $Z^* \simeq 0.036$, then formula (5.12), in conjunction with (5.11) and (5.6*a*), is simplified to

$$0.75 w_b^* + 0.105 T_o^* = 0.02625,$$

which for $T_o^* = -0.10$, as derived from (5.4*a*), yields $w_b^* = 0.049$. Thus, in conclusion, the employees would be able to enjoy a 4.9 percent increase in wage rates, a 10 percent increase in paid holidays, and a 10 percent reduction in overtime work; in the end, they would be better off in terms of total remuneration by 3 percent. The employers, on the other hand, would ensure the cooperation of the employees in increasing the productivity of labor by

1.5 percent and would improve sales and profit levels by 1 and 3.6 percent, respectively.

5.5.5. Profit-Sharing Considerations

Figure 5.10 shows the linear relationships between Z^* and L^* pertaining to the conditions described under scenarios 1, 2, and 3. It could provide the starting point for discussions on profit-sharing schemes. The final arrangement, if reached, could clearly be more elaborate than simply stating that the employees are entitled to share a fixed proportion of any profit increase. This proportion could well be dependent on the causes of the profit increase (higher, say, if the profit increase arises from $N^* - V^*$ being negative and lower if the profit increase arises from actions on prices). In any event, if the discussions are fruitful and some agreement is reached, then not only would future negotiations become easier but the employees would gain a better understanding of corporate objectives and realize that if they want to earn more, then it is in their interest to ensure that the company earns more.

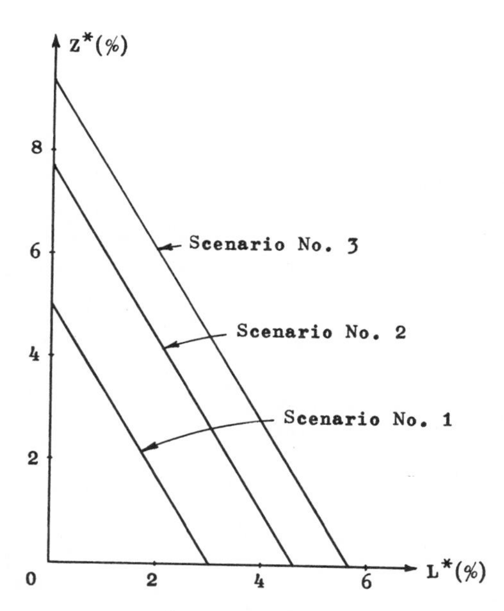

FIGURE 5.10. Relationships between Z^* and L^*: A Starting Point for the Development of Profit-Sharing Schemes?

5.6. CONCLUSIONS

This paper developed and analyzed a set of simple, interrelated, descriptive models that could form the basis of discussions on pay and working conditions between employers and employees. The models are versatile enough to allow the following:

- The use of alternative assumptions and functional relationships to reflect differing views of the negotiators;
- Sensitivity analyses to identify the most crucial assumptions and estimates that are likely to affect the results;
- Evaluation of the possible consequences of capital expenditure, or product diversification plans, or both;
- Further disaggregation to incorporate additional variables and a more detailed breakdown of working hours, wage rates, or costs, if this is thought to be desirable;
- Suitable modifications to account for other payoffs or objectives to either employers or employees.

It is recommended that such models be developed, discussed, and analyzed by the negotiators themselves in an attempt to make them highlight the issues, arguments, and important characteristics pertaining in each individual case. The models could then provide the basis of a common communication language leading to a better understanding of each others' position and, it is hoped, to less conflict. At this stage it may become feasible to extend the use of the models to the longer term. The negotiators would thus be able to discuss the possibility of reaching some broad agreement in connection with future policies on employment, working hours, wage rates, and benefits for any given set of planned or expected changes in demand, production processes, or the general economic and social environment.

REFERENCES

Cosmetatos, G. P., N. Barbaroussis, and S. Eilon, 1979, "The Status of Variable Costs in Profitability Planning," *OMEGA* 7:82–84.

Eilon, S., 1975, "Changes in Profitability Components," *OMEGA* 3:353–54.

Eilon, S., and G. P. Cosmetatos, 1977, "A Profitability Model for Tactical Planning," *OMEGA* 5:673–88.

______, 1979*a*, "Effect of Price and Allied Changes on Profit," *Applied Economics* 11.

______, 1979*b*, "A Decision-Making Model for Short-Term Financial Planning," paper presented at EURO III Congress, Amsterdam.

Kurosawa, K., 1975, "An Aggregate Index for the Analysis of Productivity and Profitability," *OMEGA* 3:157–68.

6 PERSONNEL ASSIGNMENT WITH A BUDGET CONSTRAINT

John C. Panayiotopoulos

An important problem of human resource management that is concerned with employees' productivity in a firm is undoubtedly the assigning of personnel to roles or jobs according to a given set of criteria (Childs, 1972; Derman, 1972; Nelson, 1970; Wilson, 1977; Panayiotopoulos, 1978). This problem is usually termed the *personnel allocation problem,* and it deals with the allocation function of human resource management. On the other hand, it is usually necessary for industrial units to provide education, training, and development to the personnel in order to increase productivity on the current job (Sinha, 1970; Walker, 1969; Moder and Elmaghraby, 1978). Broadly speaking, the above industrial activities appear in the course of time according to the following order:

1. There are n jobs and m candidates; if $n < m$, then choose n individuals and hire them (selection problem);
2. Assign the n individuals to the n jobs so as to maximize the total value of the assignment (assignment problem);
3. Provide education and development to the employees according to the present (short-term) and future (long-term) needs of the firm; the decision here is whether to provide development, and if so, when, for what duration, of what kind, and to whom (development problem).

In a recent work (Panayiotopoulos and Papoulias, 1979) a procedure capable of solving the problems (1) and (2) simultaneously has been proposed. Balinski and Reisman (1972) have solved a version of problem (3) by using a dynamic process. On the other hand, occasionally it is possible to apply sequential approaches, goal programming models, and simulations (Moder and Elmaghraby, 1978).But unfortunately, it seems that in many real situations concerned with employees' productivity the following difficulties always arise: Finding the data required by the above methods is unrealistic; and activities (1), (2), and (3) are not independent of each other. Therefore, a complete and unified model concerning activities (1), (2), and (3) must give a better solution than a combined solution given by the other methods. The question of such a complex problem can be outlined as follows: Select n individuals and assign them to the n roles so that (a) the total cost is less or equal to a given number, (b) the n individuals cover, from the functional point of view, all the requirements of the roles, given that it is possible for the firm to provide on-the-job training to the employee; and (c) the total productivity at the end of the first period, when the educational program will have been already completed, is maximized.

Obviously, in order to solve this problem, we have to involve activities (1), (2), and (3) simultaneously. It must be noted that the requirements of condition (b) must be concerned with the requirements of the present as well as with the requirements of the future; this policy allows whichever change to future needs of the firm.

So far, we placed emphasis on the fact that the n jobs can be distinguished. But in a number of real situations, the roles cannot be distinguished, and generally the individuals work together in order to study, research, and solve some specific problem that corresponds to some given task. This special problem, the so-called special group, is usually associated with specific rules and criteria (Panayiotopoulos and Triantis, 1980). However, in this paper we shall deal only with the general case, that is, making the assumption that the roles are distinguished and moreover that each job is independent of the others.

6.1. MATHEMATICAL FORMULATION

Consider that the firm has n positions and there are m candidates to be assigned ($n \leq m$). Let c^*_{ij} be the score or relative efficiency of candidate i on task j. If the firm wants to exclude candidate i from the position j, then we set $c^*_{ij} = -T$, where T is the upper bound of an available computer (e.g., $T = 10^{30}$). We construct the square ($m \times m$) matrix C so that

$$c_{ij} = c^*_{ij} \quad \text{if } j \leq n,$$
$$= 0 \quad \text{otherwise.}$$

If x_{ij} are $0 - 1$ decision variables such that

$$x_{ij} = 1 \quad \text{when candidate } i \text{ is assigned to position } j,$$
$$= 0 \quad \text{otherwise,}$$

then the complex activity (1) – (2) is equivalent to the following assignment model:

$$A(X^0) = \text{maximize } A(X) = \sum_{i,j} c_{ij}x_{ij} \tag{6.1}$$

subject to

$$\sum_i x_{ij} = 1, \text{ for all } j,$$
$$\sum_j x_{ij} = 1, \text{ for all } i,$$
$$i,j \epsilon I = \{1,2, \ldots m\}. \tag{6.2}$$

But it has been reported (Panayiotopoulos and Papoulias, 1979) that a number of difficulties always arise in the near future. For instance, consider that (1) candidate i is assigned to position j, (2) t^*_j is a given low bound for the firm with respect to job j, and (3) the following relation holds:

$$c_{ij} < t^*_j, \; j \leq n.$$

In this case, we obviously have to provide on-the-job training. But the development of personnel involves an additional cost, and consequently the final cost might be greater than the amount that we have at our disposal for this purpose.

Let L be the budget of the problem, L_n the cost of hiring n individuals ($L_n < L$), and a_j the cost associated with the training concerning the job j. Then we get the following constraint:

$$\sum_{j \epsilon H} a_j \leq L - L_n,$$
$$H = \{j = 1,2, \ldots ,n : c_{ij}x_{ij} < t^*_j\}. \tag{6.3}$$

Therefore, a method capable of solving the model (6.1) through (6.3) exactly must be found; but this model is an unknown one in the corresponding mathematical programming literature. Owing to this, it is necessary to involve a polynomial-time technique, that is, a method that does not require large amounts of execution time and core memory.

6.2. SOLVING THE PROBLEM

One may, at first sight, suppose that the estimation of an optimal solution of (6.1) through (6.3) is a simple task, which could be done by systematically enumerating technique, testing if a permutation of the elements of I satisfies constraint (6.3), and storing the one that gives the maximum value of $A(X)$. The supposition is certainly true for small values of m, say up to fifteen, but as the number of m increases, this method of generation becomes computationally unwieldy, because it is obvious that the corresponding algorithm runs in time $O(m!)$.

At first, we think that it would be worthwhile to consider the problem as a network design problem. Let $G = (I, V)$, $V = I \times I$ denote a complete directed graph with vertex set I and edge set V. Associate to $(i,j)\epsilon V$ the profit c_{ij} and a penalty equal to a_j if $c_{ij} < t_j^*$, and equal to zero otherwise. A feasible solution of system (6.2) corresponds to a set of cycles of G such that every vertex belongs to one exact cycle. Therefore, a feasible solution of (6.2) through (6.3) corresponds to a partition of the elements of I such that (1) each class is a cycle, and (2) the sum of the penalties a_j of the partition is less or equal to $(L - L_n)$. Additionally, taking into consideration the objective function (6.1), the conclusion is drawn that the sum of the weights c_{ij} of the partition must be the maximum possible. Clearly, the problem so defined is equivalent to the following specific multi-sequencing problem: Find a maximum-production schedule under a cyclic-production basis in such a way that the sum of penalties does not exceed a given number. We do not think that it is easy to solve this problem without using excessive amounts of computer time.

If an optimal solution X^0 of the assignment model (6.1) through (6.2) satisfies the constraint (6.3), then this solution is the optimal one of the main problem. In this case, we must provide on-the-job training to the individuals i with $x_{ij} = 1$ and $c_{ij} < t_j^*, j \leq n$. Unfortunately, this trivial case does not always happen. In practice, the usual phenomenon is that the solution X^0 does not satisfy condition (6.3).

Consider that the feasible solutions of (6.1) through (6.2) are ordered as follows:

$$A(X^0) \geq A(X^1) \geq A(X^2) \geq \ \ldots \ \geq A(X^\omega) \geq \ \ldots \ \geq A(X^h),$$
$$h = (m - 1)!.$$

Thus, the second best solution is the X^1, that is, the best assignment after excluding the maximum profit assignment X^0. In this way, we can define the third maximal assignment X^2, and generally the $(\omega + 1)$th assignment X^ω. The key idea here is that the first among the ω next best solutions that satisfies condition (6.3) must be the optimal solution of the problem (6.1) through (6.3). Therefore, the following problems must be solved:

1. If the number ω is given, find a polynomial-time technique capable of generating ω next best solutions of the assignment model (6.1) through (6.2);
2. Estimate the minimum value of ω so that at least one among the ω next best solutions of (6.1) through (6.2) satisfies condition (6.3).

6.3. THE METHOD

In this section some knowledge and familiarity with the historical works of Murty (1968) and Balinski and Gomory (1964) is required. It has been shown by Murty that it is possible to get the next best solution X^1 by partitioning S^0 by X^0:

$$S^0 = [(1,j_1),(2,j_2), \ldots ,(m,j_m)],$$

where the arc (i,j_i) means that the individual i must be assigned to the job j_i. The partition contains the following subproblems:

$$S^k = [(1,j_1),(2,j_2), \ldots ,(k-1,j_{k-1});(\overline{k,j_k})], \quad k = 1,2, \ldots ,m-1,$$

where the arc (i,j_i) means that we strike off the row i and the column j_i of C while the arc $(\overline{i,j_i})$ means that we set $c_{ij} = -T$.

Let S^{k0} be the best assignment; then S^{k0} corresponds to the next best solution X^1. After that, the new base for the next partition is the set S^{k0}, and so on. It must be noted that for the problem at hand a great number of next best solutions will give the same profit $A(X)$ because of the $(m - n)$ dummy jobs $j > n$. For instance, if S^0 gives a profit $A(X^0)$ and $j_1,j_2 > n$, then obviously a next best solution X^1 can be the following one:

$$S^1 = [(1,j_2),(2,j_1),(3,j_3), \ldots ,(m,j_m)].$$

Indeed, the following relations hold:

$$A(X^1) = A(X^0) - c_{1j_1} - c_{2j_2} + c_{1j_2} + c_{2j_1} = A(X^0) + O = A(X^0).$$

Therefore, it is necessary for us to revise Murty's partition and to redefine as *partition* the Murty's one plus the operation (6.4) as follows:

$$c_{ij} = -T, \; j \neq j_0 > n, \text{ if } x_{ij_0} = 1, \quad = 0 \text{ otherwise.} \tag{6.4}$$

A second critical point is the one concerning the store and the comparisons required. It has been proposed by Murty that a good strategy is to store all the sets S^k (old plus new ones) and to take out the one that gives the maximal profit; certainly, we do not store the solutions that we have already found, that is, X^0, X^1, X^2, etc. Consequently, it is necessary to store at most $(m - 1)$ solutions at the first stage, $(2m - 3)$ at the second stage, and $(wm - 2m + 1)$ at wth stage. It must be noted that each solution requires that a square matrix $m \times m$ be stored. Owing to this, the conclusion is drawn that the memory requirements are $O(wm^3)$ numbers at stage w. Obviously, this policy requires a large number of storage locations, a number that is greater than the limit for feasibility of processing on current computers, even when $(w,m) = (10,50)$. Owing to this, we propose the following strategy: Store only the $(\omega - \varphi)$ maximal solutions, where $\varphi = 1, 2, \ldots, \omega - 1$ is the present stage. Assuming that the number ω is given, then this strategy can be efficiently organized by sorting the new $(m - 1)$ solutions and the $(\omega - \varphi)$ old ones at stage φ, and storing only the $(\omega - \varphi)$ maximal solutions among them. Therefore, the skeleton of an algorithm for finding an optimal solution of model (6.1) through (6.3) can now be outlined as follows:

Step 1: The number ω and the matrix C are given; open the list LS, and set $LS = \emptyset$; *compute the first optimal solution* X^0, and store the set S^0; if X^0 satisfies condition (6.3), go to step 7; otherwise, set $\tilde{\omega} = 1$;

Step 2: Construct the corresponding partition, and solve the assignment problems of S^k using the method of Balinski and Gomory (1964); set instead of LS, $LSU\{S^k\}$;

Step 3: Sort the element of LS in order of decreasing profit; keep in LS only the first $(\omega - \tilde{\omega})$ solutions;

Step 4: Pick up the first solution of the list LS; let S^{k0} be this solution; if S^{k0} satisfies condition (6.3), go to step 7;

Step 5: Increase $\tilde{\omega}$ to $\tilde{\omega} + 1$; If $\tilde{\omega} \geq \omega$ then go to step 6; otherwise, set instead of LS, $LS - \{S^{k0}\}$, and return to step 2;

Step 6: There does not exist any feasible solution of model (6.1) through (6.3) with respect to the given value of parameter ω; exit 1;

Step 7: The solution S^{k0} is the optimal one of the main problem; exit 2.

An easy-to-follow numerical example will clarify the details of the procedure. Consider that $n = 2$, $m = 4$, and

$$(t_1^*, t_2^*) = (7,7),$$
$$(a_1, a_2) = (50,40),$$
$$L - L_n = 45.$$

Let the matrix C be as follows:

$$\begin{matrix} 5 & 6 & 0 & 0 \\ 6 & 4 & 0 & 0 \\ 7 & 8 & 0 & 0 \\ 4 & 5 & 0 & 0 \end{matrix}$$

Therefore,

$$S^0 = \{(1,3),(2,1),(3,2),(4,4)\},$$
$$A(X^0) = 14.$$

The solution X^0 does not satisfy relation (6.3):

$$H = \{1\},$$
$$\sum_{j \in H} a_j = 50 > 45.$$

By partitioning S^0 by X^0, we obtain

$$\{(\overline{1,3})\}, \qquad \text{profit} = 13$$
$$\{(1,3); (\overline{2,1})\}, \qquad \text{profit} = 12$$
$$\{(1,3), (2,1); (\overline{3,2})\}, \qquad \text{profit} = 11.$$

Therefore,

$$S^{k0} = \{(1,2), (2,3), (3,1), (4,4)\},$$
$$A(X^1) = 13.$$

The solution X^1 is the optimal one of the model (6.1) through (6.3) because it satisfies relation (6.3):

$$H = \{2\},$$
$$\sum_{j \in H} a_j = 40 < 45.$$

Obviously, in this case it is necessary to set $\omega = 2$.

6.4. FEASIBILITY AND EXECUTION TIME

The purpose of this work is not only the generation of next best solutions of the assignment problem (6.1) through (6.2), but moreover (1) the estimation of an optimal solution of (6.1) through (6.3) without using excessive amounts of computer time, and (2) the check for existence of a feasible assignment with respect to parameter ω.

In the literature the useful results concerned with execution times are as follows: (1) The computations required at each stage are the solving of at most $(m - 1)$ assignment problems, one each of sizes $2,3,\ldots,m$, (Murty, 1968); (2) every assignment problem of order m requires

$$\frac{m(m+1)}{2}$$

computational steps (Balinski and Gomory, 1964) and (3) to sort Ω numbers it is necessary to do $(\Omega\log\Omega)$ computational steps (Ralston, 1966).

According to the proposed algorithm, at step 3, the list LS contains $(m - 1)$ new solutions and $(\omega - i)$ old ones, $i = \omega - 1, \ldots, 2,1$. Therefore, step 3 requires the following number of computational steps:

$$T^1 \le \sum_{i=1}^{\omega} ((\omega - i) + m - 1)\log((\omega - i) + m - 1)$$
$$\le \sum_{i=1}^{\omega} ((\omega - i) + m)^2 = \left(\frac{1}{6}\right)(2\omega^3 - 3\omega^2 + \omega + 6m\omega^2 + 6\omega m^2 - 6\omega m).$$

Additionally, step 2 requires the following number of computational steps:

$$T^2 \le \omega \sum_{i=1}^{m-1} \frac{(i+1)i}{2} = \frac{(\omega m^3 - \omega m)}{6}.$$

Therefore,

$$T^1 + T^2 \le \left(\frac{1}{6}\right)(\omega m^3 + 6\omega m^2 - m\omega(7 - 6\omega) + 2\omega(\omega - 1)(\omega - 0.5)).$$

This is an important result because the polynomial

$$E(\omega,n) = \left(\frac{1}{6}\right)(\omega m^3 + 6\omega m^2 - m\omega(7 - 6\omega) + 2\omega^2(\omega - 1))$$

gives the maximum number of computational steps required in order to get ω next best solutions of the assignment model (6.1) through (6.2), that is, the proposed algorithm runs in time $O(E(\omega,n))$. However, this result extends the historical works of Balinski and Gomory (1964) and Murty (1968). For instance, if the base is 10^{-7} minute per step (e.g., IBM or CDC systems) and $(m,\omega) = (100,10)$, then the execution time is less than ten seconds.

The remaining work is dominated by the estimation of the parameter ω. We could not estimate the exact value of this bound. This task seems to be an extremely difficult combinative problem. We think that a good empirical criterion is to set $\omega = \Theta!$, where Θ is the maximum number of jobs for which the industrial unit can give on-the-job training pertaining to the available amount $(L - L_n)$. For instance, if $(m,n,\Theta) = (100,20,6)$ then a good value of ω is that $\omega = 720$; in this case, the execution time is less than thirty minutes. Certainly, the proposed empirical bound is a pessimistic one because it is obvious that the probability $P(X^j)$, $j = 0,1,2, \ldots, \omega$ (i.e., X^j is an optimal solution) is greater than or equal to $P(X^{j+1})$. However, the feasibility of the algorithm remains an interesting open question.

REFERENCES

Balinski, M. L., and R. E. Gomory, 1964, "A Primal Method for the Assignment and Transportation Problems," *Management Sciences* 10, no. 3:578–93.

Balinski, W., and A. Reisman, 1972, "Some Manpower Planning Models Based on Levels of Educational Attainment," *Management Sciences* 18, no. 12:B691–B705.

Childs, M., and H. Wolfe, 1972, "A Decision and Value Approach to Research Personnel Allocation," *Management Sciences* 18, no. 6:B269–B278.

Derman, C., G. J. Lieberman, and S. M. Ross, 1972, "A Sequential Stochastic Assignment Problem," *Management Sciences* 18, no. 7:349–55.

Moder, J. J., and S. E. Elmaghraby, 1978, *Handbook of Operations Research,* vols. 1 and 2, New York: Van Nostrand Reinhold.

Murty, K. G., 1968, "An Algorithm for Ranking All the Assignments in Order of Increasing Cost," *Operations Research* 16:682–87.

Nelson, R. T., 1970, "A Simulation of Labor Efficiency and Centralized Assignment in a Production Model," *Management Sciences* 17, no. 2:B97–B106.

Panayiotopoulos, J. C., 1978, "Combined Designs and Labor Programming," *Operational Research Society* 29:603–06.

Panayiotopoulos, J. C., and D. B. Papoulias, 1979, "The General Problem of *m* Persons and *n* Positions for Short- and Long-Term Decision-Making," *Operational Research Society* 30:917–21.

Panayiotopoulos, J. C., and K. Triantis, 1981, "Forming Special Groups of People," *Information and Optimization Science* 2 (1): 30–43.

Ralston, A., 1966, *Numerical Analysis,* New York: McGraw-Hill.

Sinha, N. P., 1970, "Manpower Planning: A Research Bibliography," *University of Minnesota, Bulletin 52,* Minneapolis: Industrial Relations Center.

Walker, J. W., 1969, "Forecasting Manpower Needs," *Harvard Business Review* 27, no. 2:132–64.

Wilson, L. B., 1977, "Assignment Using Choice Lists," *Operational Research Society* 28, no. 3:569–78.

7 EXPERIMENTAL DESIGN FOR COMPARING THE PRODUCTIVITY OF TRADITIONAL AND INNOVATIVE WORK ORGANIZATIONS

H. JoAnne Freeman and James V. Jucker

Over the past twenty-five years, and particularly during the past ten years, many organizations have tried or "experimented" with innovative work designs. Many of these trials have been precipitated by worker dissatisfaction that was expressed by means of high levels of employee absenteeism and turnover, and even sabotage. Enthusiasm for this type of industrial experiment received considerable impetus from the press's attention to the problems at the Lordstown, Ohio, assembly plant of General Motors in 1971, from the publication of HEW's *Work in America* report in 1973, and from the widespread publicity that was given to the innovative production organizations put into operation at Volvo, Saab, and the Topeka plant of General Foods (Walton, 1975*a*), among others. Katzell, Bienstock, and Faerstein (1977) describe 103 industrial experiments that included some aspect of worker productivity that took place during the period 1971–1975. Some forty of these experiments included an innovative production organization or work design, and most of the experiments indicated some kind of productivity improvement. Nevertheless, there is still considerable doubt as to the actual impact that these experimental changes had on productivity for two reasons. First, Katzell, Bienstock, and Faerstein (1977, p. 4) used a very broad definition of what constitutes productivity changes:

> Productivity was liberally defined to embrace any aspect of worker-output (such as quantity, quality, or value), or any aspect of input or cost expended to achieve output (such as labor or material costs, turnover, absenteeism, or accidents). A productivity improvement, therefore, consisted of an increase in output without a proportional increase in input, or a decrease in input without a corresponding loss of output. Most studies reported only changes either in an output or in an input, rather than in their ratio; these changes in input or in output were assumed, perhaps erroneously, to reflect productivity changes.

Second, Katzell, Bienstock, and Faerstein (1977, p. 39) note that "the limitation of many of the experiments raise serious questions about the validity or generalizability of their findings." In fact, the results of virtually every one of the experiments are qualified by one or more of the following annotations:

1. Results mixed, but generally supporting the (stated) inference;
2. Statistical significance not reported or doubtful;
3. Questionable because of major limitations of experiment.

Others who have surveyed the literature describing experiments with innovative work structures have had similar difficulties in drawing conclusions. Porter, Lawler, and Hackman (1975, p. 252), for example, noted that

> most contemporary organizational psychologists probably would argue that job enlargement is more right than wrong, and the principles of job design derived from scientific management are more wrong than right. Yet these arguments would of necessity be based mainly on personal values or on rather tangential research evidence.

And as Hackman (1978, p. 15) observed, "We are only just beginning to develop procedures for assessing the economic costs and benefits of innovative work designs and for reconciling the dual criteria of efficiency and the quality of work life in designing work systems." He goes on to say, "We do have a substantial and growing set of case studies describing successful work redesign projects, but little systematic measurement of both the independent and dependent variables associated with these studies." This is particularly true in the case of organizational structural variables, which are independent variables, and productivity measures, which are dependent variables in such studies. It is our impression that in these studies there has been considerably more effort to develop systematic measures of work attitudes and behaviors, another set of dependent variables in these studies. This almost certainly reflects the interest of the behavioral scientists who have been involved in the design and analysis of these case studies and experiments.

Our objective is to develop a set of hypotheses, a set of productivity measures, and a set of organizational structural measures that can be used in the comparison of traditional and innovative assembly operations. We do this in the hope that this information may (1) encourage more such comparisons, (2) encourage more uniformity in the studies and experiments done with innovative work designs, and (3) encourage more thought about such comparisons before innovative organizations are implemented.

Although we feel that most of what we have to say applies to any manufacturing organization, we are limiting our attention to assembly operations for several reasons. Assembly operations have characteristics that would seem to enhance any substantive differences between traditional and innovative organizations: There is a relatively high labor content, the volume of output is usually large, and in the traditional approach to assembly, the tasks are specified in great detail and the assembly line workers are subject to relatively rigorous work rules. Assembly lines have received considerable attention in the literature of industrial engineering and management science (e.g., Prenting and Thomopoulis, 1974), and most readers have a good understanding of what an assembly line does.

Another way in which we plan to limit our study is by considering comparisons between traditional and innovative organizations only where there is a recognizable structural difference in the two organizations. In particular, we will not consider differences that are due to management style alone. This stems from our desire to be able to identify in an objective manner changes that have been made in some major independent variables associated with the organizations. Management style, although undoubtedly of great importance, seems too elusive to permit objective measures at this time.

We begin with a short discussion of what constitutes traditional and innovative approaches to work design and follow this with an examination of some models of assembly lines to determine what hypotheses about the relative differences between traditionally and innovatively organized assembly operations might be derived from these models. We then discuss the approach that we advocate for the identification and measurement of organizational structural variables and other independent variables that may influence the dependent variables of interest. Finally, we describe our thoughts on measuring productivities and the importance of measuring some costs and benefits that may not be captured by productivity measures alone.

7.1. TRADITIONAL AND INNOVATIVE WORK DESIGNS

Progressive assembly lines have been prime contributors to productivity in the United States and the rest of the world since the time of Henry Ford. The assembly line combines the benefits of the division of labor that were extolled by Adam Smith, Charles Babbage, and others, with the "scientific" analysis and planning of work advocated by Frederick W. Taylor and his disciples. It is the epitome of what has been known variously as a traditional, engineering, scientific, or rational approach to work design.

This traditional approach to work design grew largely out of the work of those who have viewed organizations as closed systems that will yield to rational analysis and theory. Taylor (1911), Weber (1947), Simon (1957), and others have tended to view the traditional hierarchical organization as the most rational known means for controlling human beings, or as the only solution for accomplishing complex tasks by humans cursed with "bounded rationality." Planning, budgeting, measurement, and rule making are tools of organizational control that have received much attention from the "rational systems" theorists. Scientific management, industrial engineering, operations research, and business administration are all disciplines that bear the stamp of this rational approach to the analysis, design, and management of organizations. The rational view of organizations and management is the basis for many, if not most, of the principles and myths upon which industrial organizations are managed, and thus must be credited with the improvement in industrial output and standard of living for most of the modern world since the turn of the century.

But at the same time that the virtues of the assembly line were being sung by industrialists and consumers, the discontents of those working on the line were being observed by artists and social critics. Sherwood Anderson, in his "Lift Up Thine Eyes," an essay written in the 1920s, and Charlie Chaplin, in his film of the 1930s "Modern Times," dramatized the absurdity of life on the machine-paced assembly line. By the 1950s academics were becoming very involved in the criticism and study of industrial work in general and the assembly line in particular. Daniel Bell (1956) wrote a classic essay, *Work and Its Discontents;* Walker and Guest (1952) surveyed workers on an automobile assembly line to determine what they thought of the work ("It lacks variety," they were told); and Peter Drucker (1956, p. 165) concluded that "people who have spent 12 to 16 years in formal education are not attracted to the job of a preautomated factory, least of all to the assembly line, which socially, if not technologically, is already obsolete."

But the assembly line persists, as have its critics. "Humanistic psychologists" Maslow (1943), Argyris (1957), McGregor (1960), and others have convinced many managers and management theorists that work should be organized and managed in a manner that is quite contrary to that used in the design and operation of an assembly line. Rice (1958, pp. 34–35), in describing the principles of work organization used in his reorganization of textile mills in Ahmedabad, India, argued as follows:

> If the satisfaction to be obtained from primary task performance is to be realized, the task must be one that is recognizable and meaningful for those who perform it. Its performance must be felt as something for which responsibility has been taken. The relationships it provides must be satisfactory. Three assumptions may accordingly be made about task organization:
>
> 1. A task should be so organized that those engaged on it can experience, so far as is practicable, the completion of a "whole" task. . . .
> 2. A task should be so organized that, so far as possible, those engaged upon it can *control* their own activities. . . .
> 3. Related tasks should be so organized that those performing them can have satisfactory relationships.

These principles of work organization are more representative of the "natural systems" approach to organizations than they are of the rational systems approach. Natural systems theorists tend to view organizations as open, rather than closed, systems that must respond to an environment that may not appear to be rational and thus may defy rational analysis. Natural systems theorists have tended to put substantially more emphasis on the informal organization, on work groups, and on the attitudes and behavior of individuals in organizations than have the rational systems theorists. Much of the impetus for this interest grew out of the Hawthorne studies conducted at Western Electric Company (Roethlisberger and Dickson, 1939) and what was subsequently called the "human relations movement."

What we are calling innovative approaches to work design are usually designs that show the influence of both the rational systems approach and the natural systems approach. They retain much of the planning, budgeting, measurement, and rule making of the traditional organizations, but they incorporate these in a design that explicitly recognizes individual and social needs and tries to be consistent with these needs. Advocates of such innovative designs include those associated with the "sociotechnical systems" approach (e.g., Rice, 1958; Trist, Higgin, Murray, and Pollack, 1963; and Davis and Taylor, 1972) and those associated with the "motivation-hygiene" approach (e.g., Herzberg, 1966, 1968; and Ford, 1969).

Sociotechnical systems (STS) approaches to job design and redesign projects require that both the technical aspects of the work and the social aspects of the work setting be taken explicitly into account. The design should produce a work system as near to being jointly optimal as possible. That is, neither the technical system nor the social system should be optimized at the expense of the other. Autonomous work groups and teams are the major devices used by this approach, with the group or team members sharing decision making and the planning and execution of work. Sociotechnical analysis has been criticized for its lack of a theoretical basis and its failure to provide specific design principles and procedures. In fairness, we should add that it has produced many exciting and influential designs and that it is still being developed (Davis and Cherns, 1975; Mumford, n.d). Taylor (1975) describes the STS process and what design teams and task forces do in STS analysis.

Herzberg's motivation-hygiene theory offers a model composed of two main factors: intrinsic determinants ("motivation" factors) of employee satisfaction (e.g., recognition, achievement, responsibility, advancement, personal growth, and competence) and extrinsic determinants ("hygiene" factors) of employee dissatisfaction (e.g., company policies, pay plans, working conditions). Hackman and Oldham (1976) discuss this theory, claim it to be "by far the most influential theory relevant to work design," and add that "there are difficulties with the theory that . . . compromise its usefulness." Empirical support for the major tenets is lacking, and individual differences among workers are not taken into account in the theory. But, like the sociotechnical approach, the motivation-hygiene approach has been used to produce many work designs that appear to be extremely effective.

Leavitt (1978) has observed that jobs of upper-level managers and professionals are quite regularly consistent in much of their content with what the advocates of the sociotechnical approach or the motivation-hygiene approach would propose. But such designs have been applied in lower levels of organizations, at the level of the assembly line for example, with considerable reluctance. This reluctance undoubtedly stems from several things, among which must be counted the lack of a widely accepted theory of job design and the fear that productivity will suffer if an innovative design is implemented.

Meaningful comparisons of traditionally and innovatively designed work organizations are needed to understand what constitutes good innovative designs and how such designs influence productivity. Meaningful comparisons require meaningful measures of the design variables (dimensions of organizational structure) and the outcome variables (productivities, satisfactions, and related quantities). In what follows we attempt to provide a framework for thinking about comparisons and the measurements required to make them meaningful.

7.2. MODELS AND HYPOTHESES

Engineers, economists, sociologists, psychologists, and behavioral scientists all use models to help them design, analyze, or predict the performance of work groups. These models range from the detailed, quantitative models of the engineers to the broader and more qualitative models of the sociologists. Partly out of academic curiosity and partly to see if any useful predictions about the relative performance of innovative work groups can be derived from these models, we now make a brief survey of some of these models.

In what follows, it will help if we think in terms of a specific product and a specific assembly line. Let us suppose that the product is made in large quantities (millions per year) and is composed of approximately 250 parts. It is typically produced on an assembly line manned by about twenty assemblers using a substantial amount of special-purpose tooling. Each assembler spends approximately one-and-one-half minutes on each unit produced. One large corporation has many such assembly lines in a variety of plants. Technologies used in the newer plants are similar to, but not identical to, those used in the older plants. The innovative organizations in this corporation differ from the more traditional organizations as follows:

1. In the newer operations the workers on each assembly line are organized as an autonomous work group; this group makes decisions on work methods, work rules, training among and by its members, and the disciplining of those who violate the work rules; the groups meet as often as they feel is necessary;
2. There are no foremen in the newer operations;
3. General foremen have been replaced by "area advisors," who may be called upon for help by any of the groups with which they are associated; these advisors are usually persons with many years of experience in the older operations;
4. Workers in the newer, more innovative organizations are paid "for knowledge" rather than for a particular task to which they are assigned; workers acquire knowledge of the operation by learning more and more tasks; the group decides how many tasks a worker can do and thus what his or her wage rate will be; a worker who knows all of the tasks in a plant will receive the maximum pay possible in that plant.

7.2.1. Engineering Models

We will consider three models that engineers use to design and analyze assembly lines. Although these analyze work in great detail and permit engineers and technicians to specify an assembly line design, there are some surprising omissions in the factors considered by these models.

Motion and Time Study. Most assembly operations are analyzed using the classical procedures of motion and time study. The assembly task is studied by an analyst; then, using the principles of motion study, the analyst determines an efficient method for doing the task and specifies all of the motions required by an operator to do the task. Associated with each of a large set of specified motions (e.g., reach ten inches, grasp, lift, etc.) is a predetermined standard time. These predetermined times were developed assuming that

- The operator will be trained sufficiently so that the proper assembly method will be understood and used;
- The operator is skilled and is motivated to work at a "normal" pace;
- The work place layout and physical plant are adequate;
- There is a continuing supply of work so that the pace of the operator is not unnecessarily disrupted;
- The quality of all inputs to the assembly operation is controlled adequately to avoid unnecessary disruption.

The "standard" time required to do the assembly operation is then determined by simply adding all of the predetermined times associated with each of the motions required to do the assembly and predictable delay times. Although this procedure has been criticized on many grounds by both academicians and practitioners (e.g., Abruzzi, 1956, and Schmidtke and Stier, 1961), it has proved to be very useful in practice, particularly for light assembly operations.

The standard time is a useful quantity for comparing the labor productivity on assembly lines that are producing similar, but not identical, products. If we let

w_i = the standard time for an operator to do an entire assembly of product i,

$T_i(n)$ = the total time (labor-hours) required for an actual assembly line to produce n units of product i,

then

$$\frac{nw_i}{T_i(n)} = \frac{\left(\dfrac{n}{T_i(n)}\right)}{\left(\dfrac{1}{w_i}\right)} = \frac{\text{actual units produced per labor-hour}}{\text{standard units per labor-hour}},$$

which is often referred to as the "efficiency" of labor on the assembly line. It might also be called the relative productivity of labor (relative to the rather objectively determined standard). These relative productivities may be compared across assembly lines even though the lines are making somewhat different products.

What has been described is the determination of the standard time required to do the entire assembly. That is, the total work content of an assembly has been estimated. This is the inverse of the common productivity measure, output per labor-hour. But most of the organizational variables have been assumed away, and what we are left with is the productivity for idealized operators working under laboratory conditions. Using this model alone and accepting it at face value, we obtain the following hypothesis:

Hypothesis 1: The output per labor-hour for an assembly operation will be the same regardless of how the workers are organized to do that operation.

This hypothesis is surprising, but if we believe that the assumptions of motion and time study hold to a reasonable approximation, this hypothesis must be considered seriously. If we find these assumptions simplistic, we must either construct or find a more complete model of assembly operations.

Line-Balancing Models. Engineers designing assembly lines are faced with two interacting problems. First, they must decide the extent to which labor is to be divided. In their terminology, they must determine the "cycle time" of the line; that is, if the desired output rate is sixty units per hour, they must determine whether there should be, for example, one assembly line producing one unit per minute (a cycle time of one minute) or two assembly lines each producing one unit every two minutes (a cycle time of two minutes on each line). Knowing the desired cycle time, they then must divide the labor in the most cost-effective manner possible. Ideally, they would divide the total assembly work evenly among all assemblers, so that each worker's task, ignoring variability, would exactly equal the cycle time. Of course, it usually is not possible to divide the work into exactly equal tasks, so some work stations end up with tasks that take less time than the cycle time (no task can take longer than the cycle time without lowering the production rate). This means that some workers on the line have idleness built into their jobs. The more of this there is, the less efficient the line will be—thus, the engineer's interest in balancing the tasks along an assembly line (see Prenting and Thomopoulis, 1974).

For our purposes there are two things of interest about line-balancing models and their uses. First, the model does not include any organizational or human factors; the objective is simply to attain the best balance possible for a given cycle time, when all workers behave according to the assumptions under which the predetermined times were developed. Second, the line-balancing model shows no advantage for the division of labor. In fact, according to the line-balancing model, productivity can only decline as a result of dividing labor. If the total work content of the assembly operation can be divided into *n* tasks, each of which is exactly equal to the cycle time, then the model predicts that an assembly line with *n* workers will be equal in productivity to an organization that has *n* workers, each of whom is doing the entire assembly. If the total work content of the assembly operation cannot be divided into *n* equal-length tasks, then it would be better, according to this model, to use the *n* workers to do the total operation than to use an assembly line, which would require more than *n* workers because of the imbalance.

The line-balancing model is useful as a design aid, and it allows us to make a hypothesis about productivity on assembly lines in traditional organizations and in some kinds of innovative ones:

Hypothesis 2: An assembly line with *n* workers will be equal in productivity to an organization that has *n* workers, each of whom is producing the entire assembly.

A couple of things are worth noting here. First, this hypothesis is essentially the same as hypothesis 1. Second, even though this hypothesis may seem counterintuitive to those who know well the advantages of the division of labor, it is a fact that many innovating organizations have moved from an *n*-worker assembly line to *n* workers each doing an entire assembly. And in many cases where this has been tried, beneficial results have been obtained. But for us to understand why one would prefer either of the two extreme forms of organization of the hypothesis (or something in between), we must incorporate more of reality than we have in the line-balancing model.

An Engineering Cost Model. Kilbridge and Wester (1966) developed a model of assembly line costs that is to be used to determine the extent to which it is economical to divide the labor on the line—that is, to determine the minimum-cost cycle time for an assembly line. Their model includes four costs: the cost of imbalance, the cost of nonproductive work, the cost of learning, and the wage cost of skill. Kilbridge and Wester (1966, p. 257) describe these costs as follows:

> The *imbalance-of-work cost* results from the imperfect divisibility of productive tasks. In extending the division of labor, productive operations, which by nature are not perfectly divisible, must be subdivided into smaller and smaller tasks, and these sub-tasks assigned to separate workers so that each worker has approximately the same amount of work to do in a given time.
>
> *Non-productive work* induced by the division of labor takes the form of handling of product from worker to worker, time spent in starting and stopping work on each unit of product, and the increased communications and control necessitated by the interdependence of functions.
>
> *Learning cost* has three components: the pace-achievable cost, initial-learning cost, and recurring-learning cost. . . . Within limits, the shorter the task, the faster the potential for work pace. . . . Initial learning cost is the cost of the period of skill acquisition when the beginner in the work is producing less than a practiced worker. . . . Recurring-learning cost is the continued cost of initial learning due to employee turnover. . . .
>
> The *wage cost of skill* relates the division of labor to the deskilling of work. . . . With extensive division of labor, relatively unskilled workers can be assigned to fragmented tasks and the general skill of the craftsman passes to the system and the engineers who organize it. [Emphasis added.]

Since two of these four costs (imbalance of work and nonproductive work) increase with the division of labor and two (learning cost and wage cost of skill) decrease with the division of labor, there is an optimal division of labor, or cycle time, insofar as the total of these four costs is concerned. Using their model and data from television assembly lines, Kilbridge and Wester show that a cycle time of approximately one minute is the optimal time, and they note that television assembly lines are usually set up, on the basis of intuition and experience, to operate very near to this cycle time.

This cost model has some components that are influenced by the way the assembly line workers are organized; that is, thinking of the particular innovative organization that interests us, we can speculate that the wage cost of skill will be higher on the innovative line than on a traditional line doing the same assembly, for the members of the innovative organization are paid "for knowledge." One would expect that they will increase their knowledge, and thus their wage rate, with time. To increase their knowledge, workers must learn new tasks. So we would also expect that the learning cost will increase on the innovative assembly line. This learning cost takes one of two forms, depending on whether the assembly line is machine paced or not. If the line is machine paced, then a worker who is learning a new task will have to be assisted by another operator, perhaps a "utility" operator, until the learning worker can do the new task at the pace that is being maintained mechanically. If the line is not machine paced, then the pace of the assembly line may drop to accommodate the worker who is learning. These arguments can be stated as two hypotheses:

Hypothesis 3: The wage cost of skill will be higher on the innovative assembly line than on the traditional line;

Hypothesis 4: The learning cost on the innovative line will be greater than on the traditional line. This cost will take the form of increased utility operator time or its equivalent on a machine-paced line, and it will take the form of reduced work pace on a line that is not machine paced.

7.2.2. An Economic Model

Although what we will now describe might better be called a definition rather than a model, the concept defined is useful when discussing what is potentially one of the most important effects to be realized from the innovative organization. The concept to be defined is known as "economies of scope"; our definition will follow that of Brander (1979).

Consider a product that requires but two tasks for complete assembly. Two workers can be assigned to do this assembly in two ways: They can either specialize (each do but one of the two tasks) or they can diversify (each do both tasks).

Let

$C_s(n)$ = the cost of producing n units when the workers specialize,
$C_d(n)$ = the cost of producing n units when the workers diversify their activities.

If $C_d(n) < C_s(n)$, then, by definition, it will be said that the assembly process exhibits economies of scope when operating at scale n. That is, there is an economic gain to be realized by combining labor rather than dividing it. In the participative assembly organization, "labor" has been combined in several ways: The assembly workers do the assembly, they do the job of the foreman, part of the general foreman's function, they do some work previously done by personnel, some previously done by maintenance, and so forth. The question is, Is there an economic gain realized by combining these functions and assigning them all to a group rather than to specialists? Nothing in the literature of engineering or economics helps us to predict the answer to this question with any degree of confidence. It is even difficult to answer this question empirically. One approach would be to observe a participative group for a period of time to determine exactly what functions the group performs while producing n units. It would, of course, be necessary to observe the group over a long enough time period to get a representative sample of the group's activities. One could then observe a traditional organization to determine how all of the functions performed in the participative group would be handled traditionally. These functions could then be costed out and compared with the cost on the participative line, which would be much easier to determine.

Is it worth so much trouble to determine whether there is an economic gain to be realized by combining labor and forming a participative assembly group? We believe that the answer is yes because the question of cost comes up every time participative work groups are proposed, and thus far no one has provided a documented illustration of what the actual costs are for a participative work group and for a traditional group doing the same or a comparable task. To state our interest formally, we put it in the form of the following hypothesis:

Hypothesis 5: The total cost of producing n units will be the same for both an innovative assembly operation and a traditionally organized assembly operation.

The hypothesis is stated neutrally, since we have no theoretical basis for predicting that either economies or diseconomies of scope will be realized.

7.2.3. Behavioral Models

We will consider two behavioral models that seem particularly relevant and especially rich in their implications for the comparisons that interest us.

Behavioral Model I. Organizationally, the primary differences between what we have called the traditional assembly operations and the innovative operations might be characterized as structural. Two structural changes account for much of the difference. First, in the innovative organization area advisors are used in place of foremen and general foremen, and unlike foremen and general foremen, these area advisors act as consultants to the teams of workers on assembly lines rather than as their superiors. Thus, advisors serve a staff function more than a line function. Second, the workers on each assembly line are organized as teams, and the teams are given virtually all of the responsibilities of the foremen in the traditional organization. The innovative organization may thus be said to be "flatter" or less hierarchical, since depending on how the work groups and the area advisors interact, there are either one or two levels of management less in the innovative structure than in the traditional structure.

To individual workers these organizational changes mean more responsibility, increased opportunity for social interaction, increased opportunity for self-expression and self-determination, a better understanding of their tasks and the organization (teams must receive managerial information if they are to make sound managerial decisions), and more variety in their work. There is a large behavioral science literature that deals with how individuals respond to jobs and to job characteristics such as these. The model developed by Turner and Lawrence (1965) and subsequently modified and extended by a succession of followers is particularly relevant to our interest and should permit us to make some predictions about differences in the traditional and innovative assembly organizations. Because their work was seminal and because today's models have elements very similar to theirs, we will describe the Turner and Lawrence model in some detail.

Turner and Lawrence (1965, p. 10) describe the ideas behind their work as follows:

> The planning for this research started with the concept that every industrial job contained certain technologically determined intrinsic task attributes which would influence workers' response. By "intrinsic task attributes" we meant such characteristics of the job as the amount of variety, autonomy, responsibility, and interaction with others built into its design. We conceived of these task attributes as by no means the only relevant determinants of response to work, but as worth more systematic attention across a wide range of technological settings than it seemed to us they had yet received in existing research. We recognized that in actuality how a given worker "responded" to his job, for example, how much satisfaction he expressed with it and whether or not he was frequently absent from work, would depend not only upon the intrinsic attributes of his immediate task at work, but also upon many other influences on his behavior, such as management's policy and practice, supervisory behavior, economic and social conditions in the larger environment, pay, and his individual background, needs, predisposition, etc.

Before proceeding we should note that this was written at a time when there was much interest in "technological determinism" among those interested in organization, but even though Turner and Lawrence refer to the intrinsic task attributes as being technologically determined in the first sentence, they soften this in the second sentence by saying that these attributes are designed into jobs, a view that is consistent with innovative work designs.

Specifically, Turner and Lawrence hypothesized that jobs that rate high on autonomy, responsibility, interaction opportunities, and variety will result in greater job satisfaction, better attendance records, and fewer evidences of psychosomatic disorders (nervousness or nervous disorders traced to the job) among workers than do jobs that rate low on these same task attributes. But the relationship between task attributes and satisfaction, attendance, and psychosomatic disorders is moderated, they further hypothesized, by situational factors (company satisfaction, foreman satisfaction, work group satisfaction, pay); individual characteristics (age, education, seniority); and the way the task attributes are actually perceived by the workers.

Speaking broadly, one could say that these hypotheses were supported by the data gathered by Turner and Lawrence, but this broad statement must be qualified. First, the relationship between job characteristics and psychosomatic disorders was not established because of problems that arose in the measurement of the disorders. Second, and more important, the hypothesized positive relationship between job characteristics and job satisfaction was found to be supported only by the data gathered for workers who lived and worked in rural or town environments and not supported by the data for those who lived and worked in urban or city environments. Turner and Lawrence argued that this difference could be ascribed to cultural differences between the two groups of workers. Later Blood and Hulin (1967) and Hulin and Blood (1968) presented data to support their hypothesis that this difference is caused by alienation from traditional work norms. That such alienation is more prevalent in cities than in rural and small town settings explains the Turner and Lawrence result, according to this argument. Hackman and Lawler (1971) followed this with the idea that there is substantial variation among workers within cities and within towns and that the important attribute of individuals, when trying to predict how they will respond to enriched and enlarged jobs, is their desire for higher order needs satisfaction. The data of Hackman and Lawler and subsequent researchers have supported this position. One advantage of this is that the desire for higher order needs satisfaction can be obtained for individuals through the same kind of survey instrument that is used to measure an individual's perceptions of and responses to a job.

In a continuing series of articles (e.g., Hackman and Oldham, 1975; Oldham, 1976; Hackman and Oldham, 1976; Oldham, Hackman, and Pearce, 1976; Hackman, Pearce, and Wolfe, 1978), Hackman, Oldham, and others have developed a theory that builds directly upon the work and ideas just described. They developed a survey instrument to measure the variables relevant to the theory and described the application of the instrument and its results. Their theory predicts that jobs that rate high in skill variety, task identity (the degree to which a job requires the completion of a complete and identifiable piece of work), task significance (the extent to which the job has an impact on the lives or work of other people), autonomy, and feedback (the extent to which the worker receives direct and clear information about the effectiveness of his performance) will have the potential for producing a positive response in individual workers that will result in high internal work motivation, high quality work performance, high satisfaction with the work, and low absenteeism and turnover. The potential positive results will be realized to a greater extent by workers who have strong growth needs, and are satisfied with the work context (their coworkers, supervisors, pay, and security). There are some things worth noting about this model. First, this model is a descendant of that of Turner and Lawrence. Second, in this latest version of the model there is no prediction about psychosomatic disorders. And third, unlike the Turner and Lawrence version, the Hackman and Oldham version predicts that enriched and enlarged jobs have the potential to produce high-quality work performance.

Using the Hackman and Oldham model and remembering that individual workers in the innovative organization should experience more responsibility, increased opportunity for social interaction, increased opportunity for self-determination, a better understanding of their tasks, and more variety in their work than do workers in the traditional organization, we can make the following hypotheses:

Hypothesis 6: The innovative organization will have lower employee turnover;

Hypothesis 7: The innovative organization will have reduced absenteeism;

Hypothesis 8: The innovative organization will have better product quality;

Hypothesis 9: The innovative organization will have more evidence of job satisfaction;

Hypothesis 10: The innovative organization will have better productivity;

Hypothesis 11: Evidence supporting the foregoing five hypotheses will be strongest among those employees who have strong growth needs and who are satisfied with the work context, and weakest among those employees who have weak growth needs and who are dissatisfied with the work context.

Hypothesis 10, which states that the innovative organization will have better productivity than the traditional organization, is included because it is consistent with the Hackman-Oldham model and with evidence that they cite. It should be noted, however, that others are less certain about the influence of job design on productivity and that the evidence supporting hypotheses 6 through 9 is much more abundant in the literature than is the evidence for hypothesis 10. Perrow's survey (1979, pp. 90–138), for example, presents a very skeptical view of research related to this hypothesis.

Leavitt (1978) discusses laboratory research with communication networks which indicates that the traditional organization, which has formal direct communication only between the foreman and each worker, will be more efficient than the innovative organization, which has formal communication between all workers. However, this same research found that the morale would be higher in the innovative-type communication network and that fewer errors would be made by this group. If we assume for the moment that productivity and efficiency are the same, Leavitt's results cast some doubt on hypothesis 10 and offer additional support for hypotheses 6 through 9.

We should note that two of these hypotheses (numbers 6 and 7) predict results that if borne out by fact, will make it very difficult to determine the validity of hypothesis 4. That is, if the innovative organization has lower employee turnover and lower absenteeism than the traditional line, then the learning cost will be reduced and the increased learning predicted in hypothesis 4 may not be observable. That is, since there are two types of learning (the initial learning of new employees and the learning that existing employees will do on the new line to increase their knowledge of the operation) and since both will produce similar results (greater utilization of assistance or reduced output pace by the entire line), the results of a test of hypothesis 4 may be confounded with effects caused by lower turnover and lower absenteeism.

Behavioral Model II. Karasek (1979) presents the theory and supporting evidence for a model that allows us to make some predictions about the relative amount of psychosomatic disorders and related behaviors to be found in workers on the traditional and innovative assembly lines. He postulates that psychological strain results from the joint effects of the demands of a job and the decision-making freedom available to the worker who is asked to respond to those demands. Psychological strain and its manifestations (exhaustion, depression, nervousness, worry, tension, pill consumption, absenteeism) should be highest when job demands are great and job discretion is small, and strain should be least when job demands are small and job discretion is great.

Workers on the traditional assembly line have virtually no job discretion. The job is completely specified, work rules are rigid, and all decision-making responsibility is vested in the foreman. On the innovative assembly lines, workers have both increased job demands (because of their increased job scope and responsibilities) and increased job discretion. Thus, at first blush, it appears difficult to make a prediction using Karasek's model. But the increase in job discretion would seem to be relatively much greater than the increase in job demands. That is, job discretion increases from essentially zero on the traditional line to a substantial amount on the innovative line. On the basis of this, we predict that evidence of job strain will be less on the innovative line than on the traditional line:

Hypothesis 12: Evidence of psychological strain (exhaustion, nervousness, depression, worry, tension, absenteeism, accident rate, and visits to the plant medical facility) will be greater on the traditional line than on the innovative line.

7.3. MEASURING ORGANIZATIONAL CHARACTERISTICS

There have been several attempts by organizational sociologists to define variables that will permit the essential characteristics of organizations to be described succinctly. Joan Woodward (1965) studied the relationship between technology and organizational structure; her study generated a great deal of both empirical and theoretical work on the "technological imperative," the extent to which technology determines organizational structure. Most notable is the work of the Aston Group (e.g., Hickson, Pugh, and Pheysey, 1969); Blau et al. (1976); Thompson (1967); and Perrow (1967).

Our purpose in the measurement of organizational characteristics is to facilitate the comparison of the results of various studies of innovative organizations and to provide independent variables for those who wish to ascribe the results of an innovative design to the structural and managerial variables that have been changed.

Table 7.1 contains variables that measure dimensions of technology, organizational structure, demographics, and management. It is doubtful that all forty-seven of the variables will be of interest to any one researcher, but it is likely that those comparing one study with another would like to be able to characterize some aspects of the technologies of two or more organizations as well as the organizational and management variables.

The technology variables in Table 7.1 were borrowed, with minor modification, from the work of Hickson, Pugh, and Pheysey (1969). Although they were pursuing the technological imperative, these variables seem to be useful as a means of characterizing diverse manufacturing organizations.

Table 7.1. Organizational Variables and Their Measurements

Variable	*Measurement*
Technology	
degree of automation	
1. hand tools and manual machines	% of workers using
2. powered machines and tools	% of workers using
3. single-cycle automatic	% of workers using
4. automatic: repeats cycle	% of workers using
5. self-measuring and adjusting	% of workers using
workflow rigidity	
6. a breakdown stops all workflow immediately	yes, no
7. no waiting time possible	yes, no
8. no buffer stocks and no delays possible	yes, no
9. single-source input	yes, no
10. single-purpose equipment	yes, no
11. no rerouting of work possible	yes, no
12. a breakdown stops some workflow immediately	yes, no
13. the normal throughput is invariable	yes, no
specificity of evaluation	
14. personal evaluation only	yes, no
15. partial measurement of output	yes, no
16. measurements used over virtually the whole of the output	yes, no
work variety	
17. tasks per worker	Avg. no. of tasks/worker in the focus group
Structure	
differentiation	
18. levels of management	no. of levels
19. units reporting to plant manager	no. of units
20. subunits reporting to unit managers	no. of subunits
21. job titles	no. of job titles
personnel components	
22. nonproduction	% nonproduction at plant site
23. supervisors	% nonproduction supervisors
24. staff	% nonproduction staff

Table 7.1. Cont'd.

Variable	*Measurement*
personnel components (cont'd.)	
25. professionals	% nonproduction professionals
26. college graduates	% nonproduction college graduates
27. indirect production	% indirect at plant site
28. maintenance	% maintenance workers
29. direct production	% direct production workers
30. skilled tradesmen	% skilled tradesmen
spans of control	
31. chief executive officer	no. of immediate subordinates
32. unit managers	avg. no. of subordinates
33. subunit managers	avg. no. of subordinates
34. first line supervisors	avg. no. of subordinates
degree of lateral communication	
35. within the focus group	no. of formal channels/focus group member
36. between the focus group and other groups at the same organizational level	no. of formal channels
Demographics	
37. plant size	no. of workers
38. size of focus group	no. of workers
39. worker seniority (focus group)	avg. years of seniority
40. location	urban, rural
41. labor market	% unemployed in the region
42. worker representation	union, nonunion
43. wages (focus group)	avg. wage
Management	
44. style	participative . . . . . autocratic
45. formal communication	open . . . . . closed
46. informal communication	open . . . . . closed
47. promotion policy	ability . . . . . seniority

The structural variables in Table 7.1 were borrowed from Blau et al. (1976). We added the degree of lateral communication (Galbraith, 1973), for this seems to be an important characteristic of many innovative organizations.

Finally, the demographic and management variables are rather standard items that would be of interest to those who are comparing organizations.

7.4. MEASURES FOR TESTING THE HYPOTHESES

Five of the twelve hypotheses developed earlier can be tested using measures usually readily available from the records of a manufacturing organization. In Table 7.2 the quantities to be measured and the proposed measurements are listed for these five hypotheses (numbers 3, 4, 6, 7, and 8). Note that all measures are in units that will allow comparisons between assembly lines in different organizations even though the lines may have differing numbers of workers and output rates. Just a few comments are in order here. First, it is recommended that absenteeism be measured in terms of the number of occurrences of absenteeism in a year rather than the number of days of absences in the year because as many researchers have observed, a single long absence of *n* days is not the same in terms of the likely cause of the absences or in terms of their impact on the organization as is a series of *n* one-day absences. Second, the number of hours of rework per year is an incomplete measure of quality problems, but for many products it is virtually impossible to obtain information about failures in the field. And in many cases field failures attributable to assembly workers are small in number because of thorough quality checking. Thus, we have not included the effect of field failures. Still another problem is that some rework is caused by materials. If possible, the measure used to test hypothesis 8 should be based on hours of rework caused by labor alone, since the materials causing rework presumably are not influenced by the manner in which the assembly line is organized.

Table 7.2. Quantities to be Measured and Proposed Measures for Testing Five Hypotheses

Hypothesis	*Quantity to Be Measured*	*Proposed Measure*
3	wage cost of skill	avg. cost of an hour of direct labor
4(*a*)	cost of assistance while learning	$\frac{\text{annual cost of utility workers}}{\text{no. of workers on the line}}$
4(*b*)	pace achieved	$\frac{\text{std. hours produced/year}}{\text{direct hours worked/year}}$
6	turnover	$\frac{\text{no. terminating employment/year}}{\text{no. of workers on the line}}$
7	absenteeism	$\frac{\text{no. of occurrences of absenteeism/year}}{\text{no. of workers on the line}}$
8	quality	$\frac{\text{hours of rework/year}}{\text{std. hours produced/year}}$

Job satisfaction measures, which are needed for hypothesis 9, and measures of growth needs strengths and contextual satisfactions, which are needed for hypothesis 11, can be obtained from a survey of employees using the Job Diagnostic Survey of Hackman and Oldham (1975). This instrument will provide more information than is needed to test hypotheses 9 and 11, and it may be desirable to remove some of the unneeded items, for the survey is quite lengthy. An alternative to the Job Diagnostic Survey may be available in some organizations that use a "quality-of-work-life" survey to determine the attitudes and satisfactions of workers. One such survey that we have seen contains items that would provide almost all of the data required to test hypotheses 9, 10, and 11. Moreover, this survey form allows space for enough additional questions to fill in what is needed to complete the data requirements for testing all three hypotheses, with the exception of the accident rate and medical information needed to complete the tests associated with hypothesis 11.

Karasek (1979) describes the kinds of information required to test most of the components of hypothesis 12, which deals with the results of unresolved job strain. We have suggested that accident rate and the frequency of visits to the company medical facility may also be a result of job strain. If used, both accident rate and frequency of medical visits should be divided by the number of workers on the line to obtain a measure that is comparable across lines of different sizes.

The problems associated with obtaining the measures necessary to test the fifth hypothesis, which concerns the total cost of producing n units of product, were discussed in conjunction with that hypothesis.

Measures for testing hypotheses 1, 2, and 10 concern the concepts of "productivity." We devote considerable attention (in the following section) to definitions and concepts of productivity, for as we argued in the introduction, lack of information about productivity is one of the items that raises doubt about the effectiveness of innovative organizations.

7.5. PRODUCTIVITY MEASURES

Ruch and Hershauer (1974, p. v) say that

> the concept called "productivity" is a term that should classify and bring order to an intricate array of variables relating inputs to outputs. It could then point the way to evaluation and improvements. But to think of productivity today is too often unproductive because the term lacks specific definition and general acceptance.

Very likely Ruch and Hershauer are expecting too much from the productivity concept. It isn't likely that a few productivity measures will bring order to an intricate array of variables relating inputs to outputs. But if we can find the proper productivity measures, they can help us evaluate and improve production processes. This is not because they have brought order out of chaos but because important quantities are being measured. "Productivity" will continue to lack a specific definition that will have general acceptance because it properly means different things to different users of the term. Gold (1955, p. 9) argued similarly in his treatise on productivity when he said that

> it may be asserted that there can be no proper definition of the useful output to be compared with the input component of the productivity ratio without a prior definition of the purposes to be effected. Moreover, this principle may also be extended to the definition of the input side of the comparison. If it is then contended that the economic analysis of productivity adjustments may be animated by a variety of purposes, as is undoubtedly true, it follows that an equivalent array of measures may be necessary to support these purposes.

Our purpose is to compare the traditional and innovative work structures that are being used for assembly operations. Productivity data are important to us because the "productivity" of innovative work structures is often questioned, and although what is meant by productivity is rarely discussed in this context, one imagines that output per direct labor-hour is the quantity that is most often implied. But one of the most salient differences between traditional and participative work groups is the difference in the nature of direct labor. Direct labor in the participative work group is qualitatively different from that in the traditional group; the role of direct labor in the participative work group is extended to include much of what has been traditionally the work of salaried and indirect labor. How does one compare the productivities of these two types of work structures then? There are two very different approaches: In one, what is known as direct labor could be adjusted for either the traditional or the innovative work group to make the two consistent; in the other, the usual output per direct labor-hour quantities could be developed and reported along with the related output per relevant salary-hours and indirect labor-hours figures. Both approaches seem to provide useful information. We think that both should be used.

In addition to output per direct labor-hour, three other ratios are necessary for a reasonably complete understanding of why one organization may be more "productive" than another. The ratio of production capacity to fixed investment is an indicator of the productivity of invested capital. Large differences in this ratio from one organization to another may indicate substantially different technologies. Differences may arise from differences in age, design, or scale. The ratio of direct labor to materials utilized can help one recognize the case of an organization that appears to be very productive relative to a second organization when viewed in terms of output per labor-hour because it is, for example, substituting more expensive material for labor hours. Finally, the ratio of direct labor to the fraction of the production capacity actively utilized can help us see how effectively labor is being utilized as the capacity changes, perhaps in response to the market (product mix changes may affect capacity) or in response to investment or disinvestment in production facilities.

How each of the quantities necessary for the formation of these productivity-related ratios should be measured will now be discussed briefly, starting with what seems to be the easiest to determine, in this case, the fixed investment.

7.5.1. Fixed Investment

The capital input to the assembly process that is most directly relevant to output is that which is invested in tooling. Although building, cafeteria, parking facilities, and other items may have some effect on work group performance, we believe that the effects are small enough and difficult enough to identify that they should be ignored. The following definition should suffice:

fixed investment = current tooling cost (in 1978 dollars, for example).

In most cases this quantity should be relatively easy to obtain from company records.

7.5.2. Materials Utilized

In many assembly operations, much of the material input to the assembly process is fabricated by the same firm that does the assembly. Thus, although a market value may not exist for many of the items utilized, cost figures should be available. The definition to be used is

materials utilized = cost of materials utilized per period (in 1978 dollars).

The length of the period to be used for these measurements and the number of periods should be determined for each individual case. Although both are important for the reliability of the measurements, considerations outside the scope of this article, along with reliability, will determine the length of the measurement periods and their number.

7.5.3. Output

In the type of assembly operations that we consider, many different models of what is essentially one product may be produced on an assembly line. It is convenient and common to talk in terms of "units of output" even though several different models may be represented in the figure stated. We will follow this practice but make our statements somewhat more precise by working with "equivalent" units of output, which are defined as follows: Let

n_i = the number of units of product i assembled during the measurement period,
h_i = the standard hours required to produce one unit of product i.

Then

$$\text{equivalent units of output per period} = \Sigma_i \left[(n_i)\left(\frac{h_i}{h_1}\right) \right].$$

Note that product number 1 is the standard; that is, the equivalence is in terms of the number of units of product 1 that could have been produced if only that product had been produced during the period.

7.5.4. Capacity

In most multiproduct production facilities, capacity is a function of the product mix produced. Since that is the case in the assembly operations being considered, and since it will be desirable to have both output and capacity in the same units, capacity will be defined using "equivalent" units.

Let

H = the total direct labor-hours available per measurement period,
s_i = the time required to prepare the assembly line for a run of product i,
f_i = the frequency with which product i is produced during a measurement period.

Then

$H - \Sigma_i f_i s_i$ = the total direct labor-hours available for actually producing units,

and

$$\text{capacity (in equivalent units)} = \frac{(H - \Sigma_i f_i s_i)}{h_1}.$$

7.5.5. Labor-Hours Utilized

Three different categories of labor-hours utilized may be used in an attempt to develop productivity measures that will allow us to compare organizations that have very different concepts of what direct labor is. The three categories of labor-hours which might be used are direct labor-hours utilized, adjusted direct labor-hours utilized, and directly related salary and indirect labor-hours utilized.

Direct Labor-Hours. This is the traditional quantity used in productivity ratios. We will define it as follows:

direct labor-hours utilized = direct labor-hours actually worked during the measurement period.

Adjusted Direct Labor Hours. Since the concept of what direct labor represents may change from plant to plant, we may opt to adjust the direct labor-hours in the traditional plant in a manner that will make them consistent with direct labor-hours in the innovative plant. That is, we observe the activities of the innovative group to determine what they do in addition to the tasks of traditional direct labor. We then estimate the hours of indirect and salaried time in the traditional plant that would be required to do these additional tasks. These additional salary and indirect hours will then be added to the direct labor-hours utilized to obtain the adjusted direct labor-hours for the traditional plant.

Directly Related Salary and Indirect Labor-Hours Utilized. For both the innovative and the traditional organization we propose an "effort analysis" to estimate the directly identifiable salary-hours utilized by each organization and the directly identifiable indirect labor-hours utilized by each organization. These hours, although usually not considered in productivity analysis, are certainly part of the "labor" required for production. Moreover, this type of labor can be managed and utilized effectively or poorly, just as can direct labor.

7.5.6. Productivities and Other Ratios

In Table 7.3 we have listed four productivity ratios and two ratios of inputs that we feel would be useful in comparing traditional and innovative work organizations. The only novelty in this list of productivities and input ratios is the inclusion of two different ways for considering direct labor, the tradi-

Table 7.3. Productivities and Other Ratios and Their Definitions

Name	*Ratio Definition*	*Page Nos. on Which the Quantities in the Various Ratios are Described*
Productivity of direct labor (traditional point of view)	$\frac{\text{output}}{\text{direct labor-hours}}$	$\frac{120}{121}$
Productivity of direct labor (innovative point of view)	$\frac{\text{output}}{\text{adjusted direct labor-hours}}$	$\frac{120}{121}$
Productivity of directly related salary and indirect labor	$\frac{\text{output}}{\text{directly related salary and indirect labor-hours}}$	$\frac{120}{121}$
Productivity of invested capital	$\frac{\text{capacity}}{\text{fixed investment}}$	$\frac{120}{119}$
Ratio of direct labor to materials utilized	$\frac{\text{direct labor}}{\text{material utilized}}$	$\frac{121}{119}$
Ratio of direct labor to fraction of capacity actively utilized	$\frac{\text{direct labor}}{\text{fixed investment} \times \frac{\text{output}}{\text{capacity}}}$	$\frac{121}{119 \times \frac{120}{120}}$

tional view and the view of the innovative work groups, which results in the use of what we have called adjusted direct labor-hours. Including the productivity of directly related salary and indirect labor is also somewhat unusual, but others, for example, Gold (1955), have used similar measures in the past. Many other ratios could be defined using the seven basic measures that we have described, but the productivities and ratios listed in Table 7.3 seem sufficient for our purpose, particularly when they can be used in conjunction with the measures that have been suggested for testing the hypotheses that were drawn from the models of assembly lines.

7.6. CONCLUSION

After a brief introduction to innovative production organizations, we began by examining some models of assembly lines and by using these models to pose some hypotheses about the performance of innovative assembly organizations relative to traditional assembly organizations. We then defined organizational measures that will allow those making comparisons to distinguish succinctly and objectively the organizational types being considered. Next, we defined the measures that would be needed to test the hypotheses stated earlier, and we then developed a set of measures that could be used in productivity and other ratios useful for monitoring and understanding the effectiveness of an organization as it functions over time. One important topic has not been addressed—experimental design. In the introduction it was noted that Katzell, Bienstock, and Faerstein (1977) found the results of many of the studies reported in their survey to be doubtful because of lack of statistical significance or questionable experimental methods. Thus, there seems to be a need for a discussion of experimental design as it applies to the kind of comparisons considered here. This topic has been omitted because it seems to us that in comparison to the topics discussed here, experimental and the more directly applicable quasi-experimental designs have been dealt with extensively in the literature of statistics and the social sciences. Campbell and Stanley (1963) and Staw (1977) are good places to start for those who are not familiar with quasi-experimental design.

A point that is mentioned in the paper and that has influenced much of what has been written here is our conviction that no single measure is sufficient for the evaluation of production organizations. We feel that all of the measures we have discussed here, and probably more, are necessary for the understanding and comparing of organizations. We think that to compare a traditional and an innovative assembly organization one has to look at the wage cost of skill, the cost of learning, the employee turnover, the degree of absenteeism, the quality of the output, the total cost of the process, the satisfaction of the workers and their attitudes toward their work, the incidence of health problems in workers, the productivity of direct labor (both from a traditional and an innovative point of view), the productivity of directly related salary and indirect labor, the productivity of invested capital, the ratio of direct labor to materials utilized, and the ratio of direct labor to fraction of capacity actively utilized. All of these factors and others must be considered. And while it is possible to put a cost or a benefit dollar figure on many of these factors, a total cost figure only tells part of the story. To understand what is really happening in an organization and to be able to understand how to change, maintain, or motivate the direction of that organization, one has to look at all of these factors and decide just what is truly important in a particular instance. This approach may be cumbersome, but any attempt to understand anything as complex as a combination of people, invested capital, technology, and various organizational structures is necessarily complicated, if not cumbersome.

We hope that this discussion will promote thought, criticism, and further research in this interdisciplinary area. It is a topic that affects many within organizations as well as those in work design. We hope there will be much more work in this area.

REFERENCES

Abruzzi, Adam, 1956, *Work, Workers, Work Measurement,* New York: Columbia University Press.

Argyris, Chris, 1957, *Personality and Organization,* New York: Harper & Row.

Bell, Daniel, 1956, *Work and Its Discontents,* Boston: Beacon Press.

Blau, Peter M., C. M. Falbe, W. McKinley, and P. K. Tracy, 1976, "Technology and Organization in Manufacturing," *Administrative Science Quarterly* 21, no. 1:20–40.

Blood, Milton R., and Charles L. Hulin, 1967, "Alienation, Environmental Characteristics, and Worker Responses," *Journal of Applied Psychology* 51, no. 3:284–90.

Brander, James S., 1979, "The Division of Labor and Intra-Industry Trade," unpublished Ph.D. dissertation, Department of Economics, Stanford University.

Campbell, Donald T., and J. C. Stanley, 1963, *Experimental and Quasi-Experimental Design,* Chicago: Rand McNally.

Cass, E. L., and F. G. Zimmer, eds., 1975, *Man and Work in Society,* New York: Van Nostrand.

Davis, Louis E., and Albert B. Cherns, 1975, *The Quality of Working Life,* vols. 1 and 2, New York: Free Press.

Davis, Louis E., and James C. Taylor, 1972, *Design of Jobs,* London: Penguin Books.

Davis, Louis E., and E. L. Trist, 1972, "Improving the Quality of Work Life: Experience of the Socio-Technical Approach," Philadelphia: University of Pennsylvania Management and Behavioral Science Center.

Drucker, Peter, 1956, "Managing the Educated," in Dan H. Fenn (1956, pp. 163–78).

Fenn, Dan H., ed., 1956, *Management's Mission in a New Society,* New York: McGraw-Hill.

Ford, R. M., 1969, *Motivation through Work Itself,* New York: American Management Association.

Galbraith, Jay, 1973, *Designing Complex Organizations,* Reading, Mass.: Addison-Wesley.

Gold, Bela, 1955, *Foundations of Productivity Analysis,* Pittsburgh: University of Pittsburgh Press.

Hackman, J. Richard, 1978, "The Design of Work in the 1980's," *Organizational Dynamics,* Summer:3–17.

Hackman, J. Richard, and Edward E. Lawler, 1971, "Employee Reactions to Job Characteristics," *Journal of Applied Psychology Monograph* 55:259–86.

Hackman, J. Richard, and Greg R. Oldham, 1975, "Development of the Job Diagnostic Survey," *Journal of Applied Psychology* 60, no. 2:159–70.

———, 1976, "Motivation through the Design of Work: Test of a Theory," *Organizational Behavior and Human Performance* 16:250–79.

Hackman, J. Richard, J. L. Pearce, and J. C. Wolfe, 1978, "Effects of Changes in Job Characteristics on Work Attitudes and Behaviors: A Naturally Occurring Quasi-Experiment," *Organizational Behavior and Human Performance* 21: 289–304.

Herzberg, Frederick, 1966, *Work and the Nature of Man,* Cleveland: World.

———, 1968, "One More Time: How Do You Motivate Employees?" *Harvard Business Review* 46, no. 1:53–62.

Hickson, David J., D. S. Pugh, and Diana C. Pheysey, 1969, "Operations Technology and Organization Structure: An Empirical Reappraisal," *Administrative Science Quarterly* 14, no. 3:378–97.

Hulin, Charles L., and Milton R. Blood, 1968, "Job Enlargement, Individual Differences, and Worker Responses," *Psychological Bulletin* 69:41–55.

Jenkins, David, 1974, *Job Power,* New York: Penguin Books.

Karasek, Robert A., 1979, "Job Demands, Job Decision Latitude, and Mental Strain: Implications for Job Design," Administrative Science Quarterly 24: 285–308.

Katzell, R. A., R. Bienstock, and P. H. Faerstein, 1977, *A Guide to Worker Productivity Experiments in the United States, 1971–75,* New York: New York University Press.

Kilbridge, Maurice, and L. Wester, 1966, "An Economic Model for the Division of Labor," *Management Science* 12, no. 6:B255–B269.

Leavitt, Harold J., 1978, *Managerial Psychology,* 4th ed., Chicago: University of Chicago Press.

Maslow, Abraham H., 1943, "A Theory of Human Motivation," *Psychological Review* 50:370–96.

McGregor, Douglas, 1960, *The Human Side of Enterprise,* New York: McGraw-Hill.

Mumford, Enid, n.d., "Work Design and Job Satisfaction," Manchester: Manchester Business School.

Oldham, Greg R., 1976, "Job Characteristics and Internal Motivation: The Moderating Effect of Interpersonal and Individual Variables," *Human Relations* 29, no. 6:559–69.

Oldham, Greg R., J. R. Hackman, and J. L. Pearce, 1976, "Conditions under Which Employees Respond Positively to Enriched Work," *Journal of Applied Psychology* 61, no. 4:395–403.

Perrow, Charles A., 1967, "A Framework for the Comparative Analysis of Organizations," *American Sociological Review* 32:194–208.

———, 1979, *Complex Organizations: A Critical Essay,* 2nd ed., Glenview, Ill.: Scott Foresman.

Porter, Lyman W., E. E. Lawler, and J. R. Hackman, 1975, *Behavior in Organizations,* New York: McGraw-Hill.

Prenting, T. O., and N. T. Thomopoulis, 1974, *Humanism and Technology in Assembly Line Systems,* Rochelle Park, N.J.: Spartan-Hayden.

Rice, A. K., 1958, *Productivity and Social Organization: The Ahmedabad Experiment,* London: Tavistock.

Roethlisberger, Fritz J., and W. J. Dickson, 1939, *Management and the Worker,* Cambridge, Mass.: Harvard University Press.

Ruch, W. A., and J. C. Hershauer, 1974, *Factors Affecting Worker Productivity,* Bureau of Business and Economic Research, Tempe: Arizona State University.

Schmidtke, Hans, and F. Stier, 1961, "An Experimental Evaluation of the Validity of Predetermined Elemental Time Systems," *Journal of Industrial Engineering* 12, no. 3:182–205.

Simon, Herbert A., 1957, *Administrative Behavior,* New York: Free Press.

Staw, Barry, 1977, "The Experimenting Organization: Problems and Prospects," in B. M. Staw, ed., (1977, pp. 466–86).

———, ed., 1977, *Psychological Foundations of Organizational Behavior,* Santa Monica, Calif.: Goodyear.

Tannenbaum, Arnold S., et al., 1974, *Hierarchy in Organizations,* San Francisco: Jossey-Bass.

Taylor, Frederick W., 1911, *The Principles of Scientific Management,* New York: Harper.

Taylor, James C., 1975, "The Human Side of Work: The Socio-Technical Approach to Work System Design," paper presented at the Third Annual Systems Conference of the Hospital Management Systems Society of the American Hospital Association, Long Beach, Calif.

Thompson, James D., 1967, *Organizations in Action,* New York: McGraw-Hill.

Trist, Eric L., G. W. Higgin, H. Murray, and A. B. Pollack, 1963, *Organizational Choice,* London: Tavistock.

Turner, Arthur N., and Paul R. Lawrence, 1965, *Industrial Jobs and the Worker,* Boston: Harvard Graduate School of Business Administration.

U.S. Department of Health, Education and Welfare, 1973, *Work in America,* Washington, D.C.: Gov't. Printing Office.

Walker, Charles R., and R. H. Guest, 1952, "The Man on the Assembly Line," *Harvard Business Review,* May–June:71–83.

Walton, Richard E., 1975*a,* "From Hawthorne to Topeka and Kalmar," in E. L. Cass and F. G. Zimmer (1975, pp. 116–34).

———, 1975*b,* "Explaining Why Success Didn't Take," *Organizational Dynamics,* Winter:3–22.

Weber, Max, 1947, *The Theory of Social and Economic Organization,* New York: Oxford University Press.

Woodward, Joan, 1965, *Industrial Organization: Theory and Practice,* London: Oxford University Press.

8 MARKET STRUCTURE, TECHNOLOGICAL DEVELOPMENT, AND PRODUCTIVITY: *Some Empirical Evidence*

Ellen Susanna Cahn and Lloyd J. Dumas

Empirical investigations in the 1950s into the sources of productivity growth found that a significant part of that growth could be attributed to technological change (see, for example, Kendrick, 1956; Solow, 1957; Abromowitz, 1956; Denison, 1962). The proportion of growth accounted for by technology varies from one study to another, partly because of measurement problems and differences in data, but all agree that technology is an important factor. This spurred a series of investigations into the process of technological change. It began to be treated as an endogenous process; various factors within the firm were examined for their effect on technology.

While some of the progress of technology is undoubtedly the work of single inventors and some major scientific breakthroughs are the result of serendipity, it is also true that an important contribution to technological progress comes from the many small and large advances that are a result of the work of private firms. Some of this progress is a result of deliberate searching for new technology by research and development departments, and some of it is a by-product of the operating organization itself where technical or production personnel develop insights into alternative methods or products. From an economic perspective, it may be said that the amount of resources devoted to inventing and innovating and, as a result, the creative output produced is determined by the market demand for new technology and the cost of producing new technology. In this context the effect of economic variables on technological progress can be studied.

8.1. MARKET STRUCTURE AND TECHNOLOGICAL DEVELOPMENT: THE THEORY

Of particular interest to us here is the impact of market structure. It has often been said to have a significant effect on the investment in technology through its effect on the relevant income and cost to the firm; but the direction of that effect has been much debated.

There are two basic theories regarding the effect of market structure on technological progress. The first is that highly concentrated industries provide a fertile breeding ground for new technology. The contrary view is that the incentive to innovate arises from the persistent pressures of competition.

The former view is generally attributed to Joseph Schumpeter (1950, p. 106), who argued that large, monopolistic firms are best suited to promote technological progress. The motivation to innovate was said to be the expectation of extraordinary profits. Hence, there will be no incentive to innovate unless there is the prospect of at least temporary monopoly power. Schumpeter argued that innovation was costly and risky. Monopolistic firms would have a pool of funds available for this investment whereas firms might be unwilling or unable to take the risk if they had to rely on outside financing. Also, a firm with a relatively large share of the market will be able to reap a relatively large share of the rewards from new technology even if that technology is eventually used by all firms.

It has also been argued that some of the characteristics often associated with high concentration facilitate technological change. This is not theoretically the same as the market share argument; but it may be difficult to separate empirically. One characteristic that goes hand in hand with high concentration is large size. Galbraith (1957, pp. 86–87) has said that at our current level of technology, advancement can only be made by large, well-equipped laboratories. Also, in research and development there may be economies of scale that favor large size firms that can afford specialized equipment and a large staff with a variety of specialists. Large firms may have lower costs of financing and the advantage of established marketing channels.

In opposition to Schumpeter's view is the assertion that innovation is the result of a conscious search for new and better solutions to pressing problems and that this search activity is triggered by the pressure on profits of a competitive market. Firms in concentrated industries with excess profits would be insulated from this kind of pressure (Scherer, 1970, p. 364).

Similarly, there are possible disadvantages of size, for example, the large and sometimes bureaucratic organization structure that accompanies a large-scale research and development facility. A long chain of command must approve each project and this may slow or stifle innovativeness.

8.2. MARKET STRUCTURE AND TECHNOLOGICAL DEVELOPMENT: EMPIRICAL EVIDENCE

The argument is clearly not resolvable on theoretical grounds but the results of empirical studies in the area also vary. Early studies compared rankings of monopoly power and innovativeness. Maclaurin (1954), for example, compared a ranking of thirteen U.S. industries by important innovations with their ranking by monopolization. The rankings did not coincide and he concluded that while some degree of monopoly power is necessary for technological progress, it is not sufficient. Phillips (1956) found a positive relationship between concentration and productivity growth used as a measure of technological progress. Stigler (1956), using different data for the same variables, found a negative relationship. Allen (1969) subsequently updated Stigler's study and found no significant differences in productivity growth rates by industry concentration class.

Later studies, using primarily regression analysis, continued to point to differing conclusions. Horowitz (1962), Hamberg (1964), and Brozen (1965) found the relationship between research and development per net sales and market concentration to be positive. Bock and Farkas (1969) found a positive association between productivity and concentration. But Williamson (1965) found the relationship between research and development per net sales to be negative within each of three industries, using the leading four firms' share of significant inventions to reflect their technological progressiveness. Weiss (1963) found that market concentration had an erratic and statistically insignificant effect on productivity growth after the growth of output was taken into account. Rosenberg (1976) found a significant negative relationship between research intensity as measured by the percentage of total employment allocated to professional research and development personnel and the firm's market share.

Mixed results in the early studies led later investigators to consider the possible effects of interindustry differences. They accomplished this by including dummy variables or separating the sample into several broad classes to reflect different levels of technological opportunity. This was found to be an important variable in accounting for the intensity of research and development. When the technological opportunity variable was included, there was a weaker relation between research and development intensity and market power than without it. Some indication of a threshold effect was also found. Scherer (1967) found a probable nonlinearity between technology, measured by the ratio of scientific and engineering employment to total employment, and concentration in low and intermediate technology classes. There was a minimum concentration ratio of 10 percent to 14 percent before scientific effort was significant; the technology measure peaked at concentrations of 50 percent to 55 percent; higher concentrations were unnecessary or detrimental. A study by Kelly (1970, cited in Kamien and Schwartz, 1975, p. 5) also found maximum research intensity occurring at 50 percent to 60 percent concentration ratios. In addition, he found that concentration was not significant if dummy variables for technological opportunity were included. Using Canadian data, Globerman (1973) found that for industries with high technological opportunity there was a positive but insignificant relation.

Investigating one specific aspect of market power, Comanor (1967) found industries with "moderate" barriers to entry had much higher research and development employment relative to their size than industries with either high or low entry barriers.

8.3. A RECENT RESEARCH STUDY

Recent research by Cahn (1980) extends the previous studies by examining a number of factors that may be causally related to technological change in a framework that separates interindustry differences.

In this research three essential factors were tested for their effect on technological progress and, hence, at least in the long term, on productivity growth. These are: cost pressures; capability for financing investment in frontier technology; and, of course, market power, the variable whose effects are the focus of this paper. Cost pressures were further broken down into variable costs and a rental cost of capital proxy.

Essentially, all of the measures used for technological progress that are amenable to statistical analysis involve serious imperfections, but in different ways. Cahn used five alternate measures of the dependent variable: constant dollar R&D expenditures, R&D expenditures per net sales, R&D employment, R&D employment per thousand employees, and productivity measured as constant-dollar value added per production worker-hour.

A number of researchers have examined the relationship between the effects of R&D, the productivity measures, and the inputs into the R&D process of funds and human capital. A positive correlation was found for manufacturing (see, for example, Griliches, 1979; Nadiri, 1979; Terleckyj, 1974, p. 37).

Five industries were included in the sample: motor vehicles (SIC-371), chemicals and allied products (SIC-28), primary metals (SIC-33), rubber (SIC-30), and nonelectrical machinery (SIC-35). This industry sample includes a wide range of products manufactured in both product- and process-oriented industries. The model was fitted by ordinary least squares to annual data for the years 1958–1973.

The results for the concentration variable, the central focus of the analysis, are reproduced in Table 8.1. Out of twenty-five measurements of the effect of concentration on technological progress within the context of this model (five industries × five measures of technology), twenty-three coefficients are nonsignificant. Of the three cases in which the coefficients were statistically significant, two of them are negative and only one is positive. When a trend is included, there are three significantly negative coefficients and no significant positive ones. Thus in the bulk of the present cases, including at least one regression in every industry, there is no statistically supported evidence of any relationship between market concentration and technological development. The statistically significant cases indicate that concentration and technological development may sometimes be inversely related.

It is interesting to note that whereas the coefficient of CONCEN (variable for concentration) is significantly positive for the machinery industry regression with productivity as the dependent variable, it is negative and insignificant for the other two technology measures. This could be explained by the introduction into the industry of technology developed outside the industry. Such an occurrence could well result in higher value added per production-worker-hour inside the industry despite meager intraindustry input into the process of technological development, negatively associated with industry concentration. Thus, the output measure of technology (PRDTY) could be positively related to concentration in this industry at the same time that the input technology measures (RDEXP, RDEMP) were negatively related or unrelated. It is well known that one of the major technological innovations in the recent history of the machine tool component of the industry, numerical control, fell into this category, having been developed in the aerospace industry. However, it is beyond the scope of the present paper to investigate the technological history of machinery since 1958 thoroughly enough to confirm or deny this possibility.

Table 8.1. Summary of Regression Coefficients of the Concentration Variable

Industry	*Dependent Variables*				
	RDEXP	*RDEXP/NS*	*RDEMP*	*RDEMP/TE*	*PRDTY*
Motor vehicles	– 26.5622*	– 0.0465	– 0.2441	– 0.6523	– 0.2040
	(– 2.88)	(– 0.96)	(– 1.03)	(– 1.16)	(– 1.96)
Chemicals and allied products	– 8.8640	0.1079	1.2135	0.9235	– 0.7157
	(– 0.26)	(0.59)	(1.02)	(0.50)	(– 1.03)
Primary metals	– 2.5649	– 0.0027	0.0022	0.0341	– 0.0557
	(– 0.69)	(– 0.14)	(0.02)	(0.23)	(– 0.61)
Rubber	1.2571	– 0.0036	– 0.0320	– 0.2785*	0.0482
	(0.59)	(– 0.20)	(– 0.52)	(– 3.18)	(1.32)
Machinery	5.7865	0.0257	– 3.4489	– 0.8319	0.7215*
	(0.10)	(0.27)	(– 1.95)	(– 1.04)	(2.31)

NOTE: ( ) = *t*-statistic; * = significant at the 5 percent level.

Overall, the weight of evidence developed in this analysis is against the Schumpeterian theory that more monopolistic firms generate significantly higher rates of technological progress.

The coefficient of the profit variable is insignificant in all but three of the twenty-five cases, and those are negative. These results also seem to be counter to Schumpeterian theory.

The results for the variable cost (labor and materials including fuel) variable are even more striking. In thirteen out of twenty-five cases, its coefficient is significantly positive. It is not significantly negative in even one case. Thus it would appear that the pressure generated by rising labor, fuel, and materials costs plays an important role in decisions to increase technology development efforts.

The capital cost variable's coefficient, on the other hand, is nonsignificant in eighteen out of twenty-five cases. In 70 percent of the cases in which it is significant it is negative. Thus, it would seem that annual capital costs do not play as important a role in the technology process in the group of industries sampled as do annual variable costs. To the extent that they do play a significant role, they are predominantly a drag on that process—a result that is not difficult to understand if the relevant technologies are primarily capital embodied.

8.4. POLICY IMPLICATIONS

Behind the manufacturing productivity crisis that began in the United States in the middle 1960s lies a serious and well-documented failure of technology.[1] Our investigation has produced evidence on the impact of some of the most commonly discussed factors on the process of technological development.

Within the various limitations of the data and design, our research indicates that industrial concentration or the profitability associated with size does not contribute in any significant way to the progress of technology. What indication there is of the significance of this factor points predominantly to a negative role. Thus, on the basis of this analysis at least, it would seem that the rigorous pursuit of antitrust policy is highly unlikely to have any real negative impact on technological development and could quite possibly have positive influence. Since the improvement of technology plays such a key role in the growth of productivity, the activation of stronger antitrust policy is likely to play a role in ameliorating the productivity crisis. Additionally, policies that attempt to encourage technological development by enhancing profitability *per se* are quite possibly misguided. If such policies are to be attempted nevertheless, they should strongly tie any tax incentives, for example, to direct expenditures on well-defined research and development projects and not assume that generally increased profitability will necessarily enhance industrial R&D efforts.

The importance of the pressure of variable costs in encouraging the development of new technology would imply that policies such as wage controls, intended to counter inflation by turning down cost pressures, may be deleterious to the progress of technology. If this is so, the further implication is that such policies may lead, through the intervening technology variable, to the deterioration of productivity growth. Since recent empirical analysis has indicated that the retardation of productivity growth may have played a key role in generating inflation,[2] it would seem that such artificial wage restraint might exacerbate the very problem it is being used to mitigate. This is not to say that such policy is definitely contraindicated, but merely that it is not necessarily as obviously effective as it might seem.

The escalation of capital costs, to the extent that it has been shown to influence technological progress, appears to be predominantly negative in its effects, a situation that highlights the importance of encouraging cost-reducing, productivity-improving technological progress in the nation's capital goods industries. In this light, policies to improve the seriously lagging performance of key U.S. industries, such as machine tools, are seen to be particularly useful.

NOTES

1. The general recognition of the importance of this problem is illustrated by its treatment as the cover story of *Business Week,* July 3, 1978.
2. For a basic theoretical treatment, see Branson (1972, pp. 322–34). A recent empirical analysis is Hong, 1979.

REFERENCES

Abramowitz, M., 1956, "Resource and Output Trends in the United States since 1870," *Papers and Proceedings of the American Economic Association:*5–23.

Allen, Bruce T., 1969, "Concentration and Economic Progress: Note," *American Economic Review* 59, no. 4:600–04.

Bock, B., and J. Farkas, 1969, *Concentration and Productivity: Some Preliminary Problems and Findings,* Conference Board Studies in Business Economics, no. 103, New York: National Industrial Conference Board.

Branson, William H., 1972, *Macroeconomic Theory and Policy,* New York: Harper & Row.

Brozen, Yale, 1965, "R&D Differences among Industries," in Tybout (1965, pp. 90–128).

Cahn, Ellen Susanna, 1980, "The Impact of Economic Concentration on Technological Progress," Ph.D. dissertation, Columbia University.

Comanor, W., 1967, "Market Structure, Product Differentiation, and Industrial Research," *Quarterly Journal of Economics* 81, no. 4:639–57.

Denison, E. F., 1962, *The Sources of Economic Growth in the United States and the Alternatives before Us,* New York: Committee for Economic Development.

Galbraith, John Kenneth, 1957, *American Capitalism,* rev. ed., Boston: Houghton Mifflin.

Globerman, S., 1973, "Market Structure and R&D in Canadian Manufacturing Industries," *Quarterly Review of Economics and Business* 13, no. 2:59–67.

Griliches, Zvi, 1979, "Issues in Assessing the Contributions of Research and Development to Productivity Growth," *Bell Journal of Economics* 10, no. 1:113.

Hamberg, D., 1964, "Size of Firm, Oligopoly, and Research: The Evidence," *Canadian Journal of Economics and Political Science,* February:74–75.

Hong, Byung Y., 1979, *Inflation under Cost Pass-Along Management,* New York: Praeger.

Horowitz, Ira, 1962, "Firm Size and Research Activity," *Southern Economic Journal,* January:298–301.

Kamien, Morton I., and Nancy L. Schwartz, 1975, "Market Structure and Innovation: A Survey," *Journal of Economic Literature,* March.

Kelly, T. M., 1970, "The Influence of Firm Size and Market Structure on the Research Efforts of Large Multiple-Product Firms," Ph.D. dissertation, Oklahoma State University, cited in Kamien and Schwartz (1975).

Kendrick, John W., 1956, "Productivity Trends: Capital and Labor," *Review of Economics and Statistics,* May.

Maclaurin, W. R., 1954, "Technological Progress in Some American Industries," *American Economic Review* 44, no. 2:178–89.

Nadiri, M. Ishaq, 1979, "Contributions and Determinants of Research and Development Expenditures in the U.S. Manufacturing Industries," Working Paper No. 360, New York: National Bureau of Economic Research (June).

Phillips, Almarin, 1956, "Concentration, Scale, and Technological Change in Selected Manufacturing Industries, 1899–1939," *Journal of Industrial Economics,* June:179–93.

Rosenberg, Joel B., 1976, "Research and Market Share: A Reappraisal of the Schumpeter Hypothesis," *Journal of Industrial Economics* 25, no. 2:101.

Scherer, F. M., 1967, "Market Structure and the Employment of Scientists and Engineers," *American Economic Review* 57:524–31.

———, 1970, *Industrial Market Structure and Economic Performance,* Chicago: Rand McNally.

Schumpeter, Joseph A., 1950, *Capitalism, Socialism, and Democracy,* New York: Harper & Row.

Solow, Robert M., 1957, "Technical Change and the Aggregate Production Function," *Review of Economics and Statistics* 39, no. 3:132.

Stigler, George J., 1956, "Industrial Organization and Economic Progress," in White (1956, pp. 269–82).

Terleckyj, Nestor, 1974, *Effects of R&D on the Productivity Growth of Industry: An Exploratory Study,* Washington, D.C.: National Planning Association.

Tybout, Richard A., ed., 1965, *Economics of Research and Development,* Columbus: Ohio State University Press.

Weiss, Leonard, 1963, "Average Concentration Ratios and Industrial Performance," *Journal of Industrial Economics,* July:250–52.

White, L. D., 1956, ed., *The State of the Social Sciences,* Chicago: University of Chicago Press.

Williamson, Oliver E., 1965, "Innovation and Market Structure," *Journal of Political Economy,* February:67–73.

9 LABOR PRODUCTIVITY IN LARGE AND SMALL FIRMS

Edward M. Miller

The U.S. government has one set of programs aimed at encouraging higher productivity and another set of programs intended to affect firm size. It is important to know how firm size and productivity are interrelated since it is possible that there are conflicts (or complementarities) between the goals. Programs to affect firm size are intended either to restrict the size of the largest firms (antitrust policy) or to encourage the smallest firms (small business policy). In addition, policies intended to encourage minority enterprise predominantly aid small business. (It is unlikely that a publicly held firm with many stockholders would be minority controlled.) Thus, there are many reasons for examining how productivity in manufacturing varies with firm size (or more precisely with the sales of the firm in the particular manufacturing industry in question).

In an earlier study (Miller, 1978*a*, 1981*a*), it was shown that the largest four firms in an industry typically had a higher labor productivity than the remainder of the industry. This was interpreted as evidence of economies of scale. However, the earlier study provided no evidence on optimal firm size since the results reported were consistent with either the largest firms being the most efficient or some other size category (i.e., medium-sized firms) being the most efficient. To address the question of optimal firm size, it is necessary to divide the "remainder of the industry" into separate size classes. This is done in this study using essentially the same data source and methodology as was used earlier.[1] (However, an improvement was made possible through use of unpublished data rather than the previously used published data with its defect of having been rounded to the nearest percentage.)

9.1. THE DATA

The Census Bureau very kindly supplied for this study the unpublished 1972 Census of Manufactures data from which the concentration ratios had been calculated.[2] This consisted of the employment and value added for the four largest firms, the eight largest firms, the twenty largest firms, and the fifty largest firms for the 450 four-digit SIC classes. The firms were normally ranked on the basis of their shipments, although in a few cases the Census Bureau used the value added. From this data it is possible to calculate value added per worker for the establishments of firms of various size. For the concentration ratio reports the Census Bureau aggregates all of the manufacturing establishments owned by a particular company. This excludes the nonmanufacturing establishments such as central administrative offices, research laboratories, and distribution warehouses.

The size of a firm in this study is measured by its shipments in a particular four-digit industry and not by its total shipments. A large conglomerate whose operations in a particular industry are very small will be ranked low in that industry even though the parent firm is one of the country's largest businesses. In a related study separate tabulations were made of the total shipments per employee, with firm size measured by the total number of employees in all industries (Miller, 1980*b*).

Using this data it is possible to analyze industries on a more finely defined basis than is possible where the data are on a legal entity basis, and all the activities of a particular firm are assigned to the industry in which it has the largest participation. Since the largest firms are usually the most diversified, it is frequently impossible to tell whether observed differences between firms are due to firm size or just to the greater participation of the largest firms in other industries. By working with data for narrowly defined industries, it is hoped that differences between companies in such factors as technology or the type of product produced are minimized. It is also possible to look at productivity in industries in which most of the production is by firms whose principal business is in another industry. Of course there were certain size categories in certain industries for which productivities could not be calculated due to disclosure problems, but there was only one industry where all data by size of firm were suppressed, and this was an industry where the largest four firms accounted for 96 percent of production (cellulosic man-made fibers).

9.2. THE RESULTS

Although there were variations from industry to industry, the overall pattern was quite consistent. The productivity declined from the largest firms to the smallest. For the two top-size classes, the productivity was above average. In the largest four firms, it averaged 120.7 percent of the average for that industry. In the next four firms, it averaged 108.4 percent of the industry average. For the firms in the middle category (among the largest twenty but not the largest eight), the productivity was essentially average (99 percent of the average).

Perhaps the most striking feature of the data is the low productivity of the smallest-size category of firms, those not in the top fifty firms in their industry. On average, their productivity was 23.3 percent below the average for their industry. Even more striking, there were only seven industries (out of 394 with more than fifty companies) in which the productivity of the small firms outside of the top fifty was above the industry average (see Table 9.1). While less striking, the productivity of firms ranking between twentieth and fiftieth was also typically below the industry average (averaging 91 percent of the average).

Table 9.1. Summary Statistics for 450 Four-Digit SIC Classes

Description	*0–4*	*4–8*	*8–20*	*20–50*	*50+*
Ratio of value added per employee to industry average	1.207	1.084	.990	.910	.767
Ratio of valued added per production worker to industry average	1.245	1.108	.991	.911	.765
Number of industries in size class with value added per employee exceeding the industry average	392	274	210	142	7
Number of industries in size class with value added per production worker exceeding the industry average	380	262	207	141	16
Average number of employees per firm	2,975	1,094	488	180	20
Average number of employees per establishment	680	396	227	115	19

9.3. THE FIRM SIZE WITH THE HIGHEST PRODUCTIVITY

There has been considerable discussion concerning the optimal size of firm. Much of the research in this area has been theoretical, attempting to determine the minimum efficient plant size and then, with the aid of an assumption about multiplant economies of scale, determine the minimum efficient size of firm. There has been less effort to directly measure the costs of different-sized firms and directly determine the most efficient scale of firm. Since in many industries labor is the major factor of production, determining the size of firm with the highest labor productivity is not only interesting in its own right, but it also provides a surrogate for total costs. Table 9.2 provides a summary of the results, showing for each two-digit industry group the number of four-digit industries in which each size category had the highest productivity. It is striking that in over half of the industries (263 to be exact) the largest four firms had the highest productivity. However, as hypothesized, there were a number of cases in which the highest productivity was among the medium-sized firms. For instance, for meat packing and blast furnaces, the highest productivity appeared to be among firms ranked eighth to twentieth. These industries are frequently used as examples to show that the lowest costs are not necessarily found among the very largest firms in an industry.

The high productivities in the largest firms are not limited to certain industries. In all but one of the twenty-two digit industry groups, over half of the four-digit industries had their highest productivity in the top four firms. The only exception was among the apparel industries where there were thirteen industries in which the highest productivity was among the firms ranked fifth through eighth (see Table 9.2).

Perhaps most striking is the absence of cases in which the smallest size category had the highest productivity, except in one unusual case (the manufacture of explosives, where the five firms outside of the top fifty report only two employees). The firms outside of the largest fifty firms operating in an industry are typically quite small companies employing an average of only twenty employees in the industry in question (see Table 9.1).

A topic of interest is by how much productivity could be increased if all firms in an industry were able to achieve the productivity of the best firms. Lacking data on the productivity of individual firms, it is impossible to answer this question. However, it is possible to calculate how much higher the productivity of the average industry would be if all of its firms achieved the productivity of the size class of firms with the highest productivity. There is a potential productivity increase averaging 30.5 percent. Such an increase in productivity could not actually be obtained merely by concen-

Table 9.2. Number of Four-Digit Industries in Which the Highest Productivity Is Observed, by Size Category and Industry Division

Industry	Top 4	Size Category 4–8	8–20	20–50	50+	Number of Industries
Food products	27	13	6	1	0	47
Tobacco products	4	0	0	0	0	4
Textiles	14	8	7	1	0	30
Apparel	12	13	3	5	0	33
Wood and wood products	11	4	1	1	0	17
Furniture and fixtures	6	5	1	1	0	13
Paper and paper products	12	3	2	0	0	17
Printing and publishing	9	6	1	1	0	17
Chemicals	19	5	2	0	1	27
Petroleum and coal products	3	1	1	0	0	5
Rubber and plastic products	4	2	0	0	0	6
Leather and leather products	7	2	1	1	0	11
Stone, clay, and glass products	17	5	3	2	0	27
Primary metal products	15	2	7	2	0	26
Fabricated metal products	18	13	4	1	0	36
Nonelectrical machinery	25	9	4	6	0	44
Electrical machinery	28	6	4	1	0	39
Transportation equipment	11	4	1	1	0	17
Instruments	10	2	0	1	0	13
Miscellaneous mfg. goods	11	7	2	0	0	20
Total	263	110	50	25	1	449

trating all production in the size category with the highest productivity. In many cases the firms in one size category are producing products of a type or a lot size that could not be produced efficiently using the technology used in the most productive size category. In particular, the smallest firms are often producing specialized products in small lot sizes that could not be produced economically using the automated methods used by the firms with the highest labor productivities.

Still, this study does show the presence of substantial numbers of firms too small to achieve the high productivity characteristic of the larger firms in their industry. It is interesting to try to measure the size of this sector. By summing the employment in all firm sizes smaller than the size category with the highest productivity, it is found that there are 11.2 million employees in establishments of firms whose level of output may be too small for maximum productivity. This is 53 percent of all employees in manufacturing establishments. Even allowing for the statistical problems in this methodology, it appears that a very substantial fraction of manufacturing is conducted in firms of less than optimal scale.

A similar calculation can be done for firms of a size larger than that for which the highest productivity is observed. Such firms are found to employ 2.6 million workers (or 14 percent of all manufacturing employees). It is harder to argue that the firms included in this group are of excessive scale since they always have the option of decentralizing by dividing themselves administratively into several operating groups and then having each part act as if it were an independent firm.

9.4. STATISTICAL PROBLEMS

There are several obvious statistical problems in the techniques used here. As the author has shown elsewhere (Miller, 1977), standard econometric methods are biased against showing evidence of economies of scale. The problem can best be understood by assuming that there are economies of scale. What one would like to do is conduct an experiment in which firms of widely differing size were established and then their costs measured. The observed data do not correspond to the outcome of such an experiment because most of the high-cost firms were either never started (once their potential owners made estimates of their likely profitability) or have since gone out of business. Thus the group of small firms actually observed consists of a disproportionate number of firms with lower than average costs either because of random factors or an emphasis on segments of the market in which they can realize higher than normal prices. Since firms with lower than average productivity are much more likely to go out of business than firms with above average productivity, the observed sample of firms is a biased sample, and the bias is most serious for the small high-cost firms. The result is to understate the effect of firm size on productivity.

Another source of bias arises because at any given time some firms are having a temporary dip in shipments due to poor sales, a strike, or a similar factor. Such a decline in output below normal usually results in a decline in productivity. Employment declines less than production because of indivisibilities in overhead personnel and because firms avoid laying off workers and then rehiring them. The smaller size classes have a disproportionate number of firms enduring a temporary reduction in shipments and consequent low productivity. The grouping of firms tends to reduce the importance of this bias. Usually, a firm is far enough from the boundaries of its size group that temporary dips in business do not change the classification of the firm. However, there must be exceptions. For instance, the group of firms outside the top fifty probably contain one or more firms that would be in the next largest size class except for a temporary dip in their shipments.

That this might be a problem is suggested by the finding that the average number of hours worked by production workers in the firms outside of the largest fifty was only 96 percent of the average for their industry. Unfortunately, it is not known whether the firms working below the normal number of hours were firms that normally had shorter work weeks, or whether firms were working short hours because of a decline in business.

The Census Bureau did not mail report forms to single-establishment firms believed to have less than ten employees (based on tax records) but took data on payrolls, sales, and industry classification from records of the Internal Revenue Service and the Social Security Administration. Data on value added and other items were estimated. The firms affected by this procedure accounted for only 1.2 percent of value added. However, they may account for somewhat more of the value added in the smallest size category of firms. Since the estimates were based on industry averages, the effect of this bias is to raise slightly the productivity for the smallest size category of firms.

The number of employees excludes unpaid proprietors and family members, while the value added would include their output. The effect is to raise the productivity of very small firms. Since the last two biases overstate the productivity of the very small firms, their low productivity is all the more striking.

There is a possibility of bias arising because large firms are more likely to be vertically integrated. The Census Bureau requested industries to report net selling values, f.o.b. plant. Multiunit companies were instructed to report for each economic establishment as if it were a separate economic unit. "Since there is no advertising or other selling costs involved, it would be expected that the value per unit of such transfers would be less than that for commercial sales" (Bureau of the Census, 1976). If firms followed the instructions, the effect would probably be to understate the productivity of the largest firms. However, a Census Bureau study of large firms showed that only about half of the firms follow the instructions, with the remainder using higher prices reflecting either commercial prices or invoice prices. It is expected that shipments by smaller, nonintegrated firms are more often based on actual sales prices and, hence, included selling expenses (and perhaps freight). It is plausible that sales expenses are higher on small orders and that smaller firms sell in smaller lots than large firms. The sales employees are nonproduction workers and frequently located outside of the manufacturing establishment.

Although a certain amount of interest attaches to labor productivity per se, much of the interest in the topic arises from the possibility of using it as a surrogate for total factor productivity. While it would be desirable to measure total factor productivity, the available data do not include a measure of the capital stock at the four-digit level. Fortunately, for most industries the labor cost is greater than the capital costs, and plausible differences in capital intensity probably will not change conclusions drawn from labor productivity. However, this is obviously an area where further research would be useful.

A potentially serious source of bias is the exclusion of nonproduction establishments such as central administrative offices, laboratories, and warehouses. These are excluded from the published statistics because it is not known which industries they should be assigned to. However, it is likely that as a company gets smaller, more and more of the administrative, selling, and distribution functions are performed in the manufacturing plants rather than in separate locations. The result could be an understatement of the productivity of the smaller firms. This problem is likely to be more serious when comparing small firms (often single establishment firms that often conduct all of their activities from one location) with medium-sized firms than in comparing medium sized-firms with the largest firms.

9.5. VALUE ADDED PER PRODUCTION WORKER MAN-HOUR

Because of the potential bias described above, the value added per production worker man-hour was also calculated. The number of production worker man-hours was obtained by multiplying the published concentration ratios for production worker man-hours (the percentage of production worker man-hours provided by that size class) by the total number of production workers. Because the published data were rounded off to the nearest percentage, the accuracy of this measure of productivity is less than that for the value added per worker. Still it is a useful check on the earlier results.

Generally, the results obtained using this measure paralleled those calculated for output per worker. Table 9.1 shows the productivities as a percentage of the average for each industry. As can be seen, the largest four firms show a productivity averaging 24.5 percent above the average for their industries, and the next four firms have a productivity approximately 11 percent above the averages for their industry. Looking at the smallest firms, it is found that the firms outside the top fifty have a productivity averaging 23.3 percent below their industry averages, and the firms ranked between twentieth and fiftieth average 9 percent below.

Another interesting statistic is the number of industries in which companies in a particular size class are found to have a productivity above the average for their industry. Again, it is found that in 380 industries, the top four firms have such high productivity, while only sixteen of the industries have such high productivity for firms outside the largest fifty. A comparison of the two measures of productivity is shown in Table 9.1. The two measures appear to give quite similar results.

9.6. CONCLUSIONS

Productivity increases with firm size in most industries. Typically, the largest firms show the greatest productivities. However, in a substantial number of industries, the highest productivity is observed for a size class of firms somewhere between the largest and the smallest. In virtually all cases, the smallest firms (those not within the largest fifty firms) were observed to have below average productivity.

The policy implications of the work appear to be twofold. In the area of antitrust policy, it is likely that measures to restrict the market share of firms will frequently discourage productivity. As pointed out in an earlier paper (Miller, 1978*b*), one of the reasons for this is that there are frequently economies of scale at the plant level, and large firms typically operate large plants. Table 9.1 presents data on the average number of employees per company and per establishment for the different size classes. It can be seen that the size of the establishment is very closely related to the total employment of the owning company in the industry. Such data suggest (but do not prove) that measures to limit company size in an industry will also limit the size of its establishments. This in turn may limit the realization of any economies of scale that exist at the plant level. One of the advantages of large firms is that they can build new plants of optimal scale without adding more capacity than they can use in the short run and without incurring an excessive risk exposure.

This research appears to have major implications for policy towards small business. On the one hand, the typically low productivity in small-scale manufacturing presents a problem for small business that might be helped by government programs. On the other hand, the low productivity observed in small-scale manufacturing suggests that programs to subsidize small manufacturing firms will encourage firms too small to be efficient, a situation resulting in a substantial penalty in terms of a reduction in national income. Since there is evidence that wages are lower in small manufacturing companies (see Miller, January 1978, 1981), such subsidies for small business may not be in the interest of the wage earners.

NOTES

1. The research reported here was done while the author was with the Department of Commerce. The views expressed are not necessarily those of either the American Productivity Center or the Department of Commerce.
2. The unpublished data were used merely because they permitted a somewhat higher degree of accuracy. Essentially, the same data can be calculated from the published concentration ratio data of the U.S. Census, 1972 (U.S. Bureau of the Census, 1975), by multiplying the totals by the appropriate concentration ratios. Because the percentages are rounded to the nearest whole number, this procedure would involve some loss of accuracy.

REFERENCES

Edward M. Miller, 1977, "Selection Bias in the Estimation of Cost and Production Functions," *Journal of Economics and Business,* Fall.

———, 1978*a,* "The Extent of Economies of Scale: The Effects of Firm Size on Labor Productivity and Wage Rates," *Southern Economic Journal,* January.

———, 1978*b,* "Size of Firm and Size of Plant," *Southern Economic Journal,* April.

———, 1980, "Labor Productivity in Small and Large Enterprises," *American Journal of Small Business,* Fall.

———, 1981*a*, "What Do Labor Productivity Data Show about Economies of Scale: Comment," *Southern Economic Journal,* January.

———, 1981*b*, "Manufacturing Wages as a Function of Firm Size and Concentration," *Antitrust Bulletin.*

U.S. Bureau of the Census, 1975, *Census of Manufactures, 1972,* Special Report Series: Concentration Ratios in Manufacturing, MC72(SR)-2, Washington, D.C.: Gov't. Printing Office.

———, 1976, *Census of Manufactures, 1972,* vol. 2, Industry Statistics, Pt. 1, SIC Major Groups 20–26, Washington, D.C.: Gov't. Printing Office, pp. xxv–xxvi.

III SOME PRODUCTIVITY ISSUES IN PUBLIC ORGANIZATIONS

10 IMPROVING PUBLIC SECTOR PRODUCTIVITY THROUGH COMPETITION

Emanuel S. Savas

It is obvious that government regulatory and fiscal actions greatly influence the productivity of the private sector. This paper will focus not on those effects but rather on the more direct effect of government on productivity. After all, government is a large and visible component of the American economy. The 78,000 governments in the United States have expenditures that together amount to one-third of the gross national product. One out of five workers in the civilian, nonagricultural work force is employed by government. Thus, the productivity of this sector will have a significant effect on the overall productivity of the nation.

Ordinarily, grumbling about taxes is a normal, time-honored, cathartic pastime of citizens in a democracy. Recently, however, the traditional complaints have been sharpened to a cutting edge. Polls show that Americans consider much of their tax money to be wasted. Proposition 13 in California symbolized this dissatisfaction and gave it tangible expression. Like parents cutting back the allowance of a spendthrift child, citizens reduced their taxes and gave their public officials less money to play with.

The high cost of government is widely perceived to be in large part due to low productivity of government services. Now there are many reasons why relatively low productivity is to be expected. The goals of government programs are not clear, and different decisionmakers have different goals in mind for the same program. Furthermore, even when there is reasonable consensus about the goals, measuring a program's achievements may be difficult, due to the somewhat intangible nature of many of the goals and the difficulty of measurement. What is the goal of a school? To equip a child for further education? To prepare a child for the world of work? To enable a child to participate effectively as a member of a heterogeneous society? To acculturate the child? All of the above? And how do you measure the extent to which any of these goals is attained?

There are other impediments to greater productivity in government. Civil service systems, originally introduced to assure that the public work force was comprised primarily of the most meritorious workers, have mostly deteriorated into blindly administered personnel regulations whose cumulative effect has been to eliminate any effective link between a worker's job performance and his rewards (Savas and Ginsberg, 1973).

This paper will concentrate on another important factor that contributes to inefficiency in government, the monopoly character of many government service agencies. Public services are often supplied by government bureaus that, for all practical purposes, have a nearly permanent monopoly in the provision of the service. This is particularly evident in the commonplace services usually provided by local governments, such as police, fire, ambulance, traffic control, and mass transit. The problem with monopolies, of course, is that they extract monopoly profits unless they are regulated, and regulation of monopolies is difficult to effect in any event. In the case of public agencies, the executives and the workers benefit by the exercise of their monopoly powers, and the public at large is the loser.

Consideration of the underlying properties of public services reveals that many of them can be supplied to the public by a variety of mechanisms, and that a monopolistic government bureau is not the only possible delivery system.

10.1. ALTERNATIVE ORGANIZATIONAL ARRANGEMENTS FOR DELIVERING SERVICES

10.1.1. Government Service

I use the term government service to denote the delivery of a service by a government agency using its own employees. Examples of municipal, county, state, and federal government services abound, and it is not necessary to elaborate further.

10.1.2. Intergovernmental Contracts

A government can hire or pay another government to supply a service. A local school district does just that when, lacking a high school of its own, it arranges to send its pupils to the high school in a neighboring town and pays the latter jurisdiction for the service. It is also commonplace for small communities to purchase library, recreation, and fire-protection services from a specialized government unit that sells its service to several general-purpose governments in the area. Counties sometimes contract with cities and pay the latter to maintain county roads within city limits. We refer to such institutional arrangements as intergovernmental contracts.

Intergovernmental contracting is by no means rare. A 1973 survey of 2,248 municipalities in the United States revealed that 61 percent had formal or informal agreements for the provision of services to their citizens by other government units. Furthermore, 43 percent of all cities produced services for other governments (Zimmerman, 1973, Table 3/1). Services commonly provided under intergovernmental contracts include water supply, sewage treatment, jails, landfills, resource recovery plants, and mutual aid for civil defense, fire, and police protection.

10.1.3. Contract or Purchase of Services

Governments contract not only with other governments but also with private firms and nonprofit organizations for delivery of goods and services. Defense contracts are a major expenditure item for the federal government and are used not only for equipment and for think-tank services but even for direct defense activities. A private contractor mans and operates the Distant Early Warning line that detects airplanes and missiles coming toward North America over the Arctic Ocean. Mercenary troops have been used since ancient times and are still being used today in clandestine wars. Even private air forces have come into being in recent years to engage in war under contract.

At the municipal level, private firms provide more benign services under contract. No comprehensive information is available on the amount of money spent by municipal governments for contract services, but Table 10.1 shows the number of cities out of a total sample of 2,248 cities that contract with private, profit-making firms for the indicated services.

The first thing that strikes one upon seeing Table 10.1 is the extraordinarily lengthy and incredibly diverse list of services available by contract from private firms. No less than sixty-six services were identified in that

Table 10.1. Number of Cities Using Private Firms to Supply Municipal Services under Contract

Service	*Number of Cities Contracting with Private Firms*
Assessing	31
Payroll	60
Tax collection	23
Treasury functions	14
Utility billing	99
Election administration	7
Legal services	172
Licensing	4
Microfilm services	41
Personnel services	6
Public relations	27
Records maintenance	8
Registration of voters	2
All public health services	4
Air pollution abatement	1
Alcoholic rehabilitation	8
Ambulance services	151
Animal control	92
Cemeteries	44
Hospitals	54
Mental health	21
Mosquito control	12
Noise abatement	2
Nursing services	33
Water pollution abatement	4
Welfare	1
General development	10
Housing	7
Industrial development	24
Irrigation	5
Mapping	67
Planning	84
Soil conservation	4

SOURCE: Derived from Zimmerman (1973, Table 3/1).

Table 10.1. Cont.'d.

Service	*Number of Cities Contracting with Private Firms*
Urban renewal	6
Zoning and subdivision control	16
Parks	4
Recreational facilities	6
Crime laboratory	5
Patrol services	2
Police communications	5
Traffic control	4
Jails and detention homes	1
Juvenile delinquency programs	3
All fire services	9
Fire communications	4
Fire prevention	2
Training of firemen	2
Civil defense communications	2
Bridge construction and maintenance	24
Building and mechanical inspection	7
Electrical and plumbing inspection	16
Electricity supply	234
Engineering services	234
Refuse collection	309
Sewage disposal	18
Sewer lines	13
Snow removal	19
Solid waste disposal	128
Street construction and maintenance	56
Street lighting	280
Water supply	77
Water distribution system	62
Special transportation services	45
Management service for publicly owned transit	18
Libraries	14
Museums	12

NOTE: Based on responses of 2,248 cities to a mail survey.

survey, and yet even this list is not complete: custodial services for government buildings and grounds are also obtained through this arrangement, and so are lunchroom operations in schools and government office buildings; tree pruning, planting, grass mowing, lawn and golf-course maintenance, weed abatement, and other horticultural services; traffic-signal maintenance, towing away of illegally parked and abandoned automobiles, traffic striping and marking, parking-lot operation, school bus transportation, and vehicle maintenance; street sweeping and leaf collection; maintenance of communication equipment, data-processing services, and test scoring; laundry services; water-meter maintenance; and management consulting. Such social services as day care, foster-home care, group-home care, adoption, institutional care, rehabilitative services, family counseling, child protection, and homemaker services are obtained by state and local government contracts with private firms and nonprofit institutions (Fisk, Kiesling, and Muller, 1978). (In 1976, of the $750 million spent for social services under Title XX of the Social Security Act, at least a third went to private organizations for the purchase of such services [Pacific Consultants, 1978]).

As noted in the table, specialized police services such as crime laboratories and police communications are procured by contract, but to a limited extent patrol services, too, have been provided in parks, public housing projects, airports, and schools through contracting, and so have investigative services to combat organized crime and narcotics distribution (Fisk, Kiesling, and Muller, 1978).

Recent data on refuse collection show that 21 percent of U.S. cities contract with private firms for this service (Savas, 1977*a*). A study of twenty-six municipal services in eighty-four California cities found that city departments produced only 50 percent of these services, while contracts with private firms accounted for 20 percent, and intergovernmental contracts with counties and special districts accounted for 15 percent and 10 percent, respectively (Kirlin, Ries, Sonenblum, 1977, p. 116).

Interesting examples of contracting for services can be found abroad. Most of the cities in Denmark contract with a single private firm for fire and ambulance services; the majority of the population of the country receives protection through this arrangement. About two-thirds of the people in Sweden get their fire-protection services from private enterprises under contract to government (Bish and Warren, 1972). And while Wall Street is cleaned by a government bureaucracy, the streets in Communist Belgrade are cleaned by a worker-owned enterprise that has a contract from the city government.

10.1.4. Franchises

Franchising is another institutional structure used for providing services. An exclusive franchise is an award of monopoly privileges to a private firm to supply a particular service, usually with price regulation by a government agency. Nonexclusive or multiple franchises can also be awarded, as in the case of taxis. In franchise service, as in contract service, government is the arranger and a private firm is the producer of the service; however, the two can be distinguished by the means of payment to the producer. Government pays the producer for contract services, but the consumer pays the producer for franchise service.

The franchise arrangement is particularly suitable for providing common utilities such as electric power, gas and water distribution, telephone service, cable television, and bus transportation. Note that many of these services are provided directly by government in some jurisdictions: Local governments own and operate many electric plants, water supply systems, and bus lines, for example, and in Anchorage, Alaska, the telephone system is a municipal service. Concessions in parks, stadiums, airports, and other public properties are also franchises.

10.1.5. Grants

Toll goods and private goods whose consumption is to be encouraged can be subsidized and provided through two different structural arrangements, grants or vouchers. Under a grant system, the subsidy is given by government to the producer, typically by direct grants of money but often by grants of tax-exempt status. An example of this arrangement is the government-induced provision of low-cost housing by the private real-estate industry. The intended effect of such grants is to reduce the price of the service for certain eligible consumers, who can then go into the marketplace and purchase for themselves from the subsidized producers more of the service than they could otherwise afford to consume.

Cultural institutions and performing arts groups are among the latest beneficiaries of government grants, a situation that reflects a recent determination that these goods benefit the public at large and therefore their availability should be encouraged by subsidies to theater groups, symphony orchestras, opera companies, dance ensembles, and museums.

10.1.6. Vouchers

The voucher system is also designed to encourage the consumption of particular goods by a particular class of consumers. However, unlike the grant system, which subsidizes the producer and restricts the consumer's choice to the subsidized producers only, the voucher system subsidizes the consumer and permits the latter to exercise relatively free choice in the marketplace.

Food stamps are an example of a voucher system. Instead of setting up a whole new government-run food-distribution system to give away food to eligible poor recipients, the latter are supplied with vouchers that they can use in ordinary, existing food stores. The vouchers are purchased at a discount, so that a person might pay five dollars and receive vouchers good for ten dollars' worth of merchandise, for example. The consumer is strongly motivated to shop wisely and to look for bargains because his money will then go farther and he can buy more; his behavior as a subsidized consumer should be indistinguishable from that of an unsubsidized consumer.

The GI Bill of Rights after World War II featured a voucher system that enabled veterans to attend college by giving them, in effect, tuition money. Note the profound difference between this approach and a grant system as epitomized by a state university. The latter is a government-run institution where public funds are given to professors and administrators to dispense education services to eligible consumers. On the other hand, under the GI bill tuition money was given to the student to spend in the college of his choice. Of course, only accredited institutions could provide education services to veterans; fly-by-night schools were not eligible purveyors of that good, and a veteran attending such a school did not receive his tuition stipend.

Voucher systems have also been introduced for cultural activities, as an alternative to the grant system. Instead of giving grants to theaters, cultural vouchers are given to individuals to encourage their attendance, and the voucherholder can attend the performance of his choice. The theater takes his voucher and is reimbursed for it (Bridge, 1977).

10.1.7. Market System

In the market system, the consumer himself arranges for service and selects the producer, which is a private firm. Government is not involved in the transaction in any significant way, although it may establish service standards. For example, a not uncommon arrangement in American cities for refuse collection is mandatory private collection, by which the municipal government establishes a requirement that all households have their refuse collected at least once a week, let's say, but it is left up to each household to select and pay a private firm to provide this service.

10.1.8. Voluntary Service

Many services that in some communities are provided as government services are available in other communities through a voluntary arrangement. Examples are recreation facilities, street cleaning, protective patrol, and fire protection. In this arrangement, the voluntary association either produces the service directly, using its members as workers, or hires and pays a private firm to do the work.

There is little information available as to the extent to which voluntary arrangements are utilized, except for volunteer fire departments; these constitute more than 90 percent of all fire departments in the United States (Fisk, Kiesling, Muller, 1978).

10.1.9. Self-Service

The most basic delivery mode of all is self-service. Protection against fire and theft is obtained primarily by rudimentary self-service measures, such as extinguishing cigarettes and locking doors. The individual who brings his newspapers to a recycling center, treats his own cold, bandages a cut, or gives vocational guidance to his child is practicing self-service. The family as a self-service unit is the original and most efficient department of health, education, and welfare. It provides a wide range of vital services to its members, and an increasing number of families are braving formidable bureaucratic forces by teaching children at home instead of sending them to school (*Time,* December 4, 1978, p. 78).

10.1.10. Multiple Arrangements

It should be pointed out that more than one arrangement can be employed by the same jurisdiction for the same service. For example, in Indianapolis five different arrangements are utilized for the collection of residential refuse: municipal service, contract service, voluntary service, free market, and self-service (Savas, 1977*a*). Not only is there nothing necessarily wrong with using multiple structures simultaneously for the same service, but if comparisons and competition are encouraged among the different service producers, the result may well be superior performance of that service in that city.

10.2. PRODUCTIVITY COMPARISONS

These various service-delivery mechanisms each have advantages and disadvantages and can be used to supply certain kinds of public service. A comparative analysis of these different modes is discussed elsewhere (Savas, in preparation). For our purpose here it is sufficient to inquire whether contracting for a service, because it offers periodic competition between service producers, is more efficient than a government-produced service, which can fairly be characterized as a long-term monopoly.

This question can best be answered empirically by reference to particular services. One that lends itself to quantitative analysis and, indeed, has been studied extensively in various settings is residential refuse collection.

The evidence is quite clear: Contract collection is more efficient than municipal collection. This has been determined by detailed studies covering the United States, Canada, and Switzerland, as well as regional studies in Connecticut and the midwestern United States (Savas, 1979*a*). Municipal collection is 29 to 37 percent more costly than contract collection, and the reasons are attributed to (1) the use of more men to do the same amount of work; (2) more absences by the workers; and (3) the use of less productive vehicles.

The disparity between the two organizational forms would be even greater if one were to take into account the fact that the comparison was made between the *cost* of municipal collection and the *price* of contract collection. As this latter includes both profits and taxes, if the contract price were adjusted by excluding these factors in order to put the comparison on an equal footing, the data would show the cost of municipal service to be 61 to 71 percent greater than the cost of contract collection (Stevens, 1977, p. 137).

When confronted with these findings, some city officials say, in effect, "We are less productive than private contractors because we employ more workers. But if we became efficient and reduced the size of our work force, those laid off would be unemployed and would go on welfare, so this city would be worse off." But surely a full employment program whose foundation is low productivity in government is wasteful. Government programs should be run as productively as possible, and if more jobs in government are to be created as a matter of public policy—"government as the employer of last resort''—all well and good: The additional workers should be assigned so as to provide additional services: they should not be assigned to perform the existing services in a less productive manner.

10.3. INTRODUCING COMPETITION TO INCREASE PRODUCTIVITY

Governments can introduce competition to increase their productivity. They can do so by contracting—under competitive conditions—with private firms to service a portion of the community while continuing to service the remainder with a government agency. In refuse collection, the experience of the city of Minneapolis is particularly important to note. Starting in 1971, half the city was serviced by the municipal sanitation department and the other half by a private contractor. Initially, the private contractor was far more efficient than the city agency. However, the city systematically compared the relative performance of the private contractor with its own department, publicized the comparisons, and succeeded in creating a constructively competitive climate between the two organizations. In this manner, the city pressured its own agency to improve its operations and to emulate the superior performance of the private firm. Gradually, after several years, the city department adopted some of the productive techniques of the private firm and ultimately reached the point where it was as efficient (Savas, 1977*b*).

One more reason why more cities do not utilize contract services is that they do not know the true cost of their municipal service and therefore cannot compare it with a contract alternative. Conventional city budgets, which are not designed as cost-accounting documents, generally do not reveal the full cost of a service under the name of the relevant department. As a result, the budgeted amount understates the true cost of the service. For example, it was found that municipal refuse collection costs 30 percent more, on average, than the cost stated in the budget (Savas, 1979*b*).

It should go without saying that contracting for services will work only for those services whose provision can be specified clearly and unambiguously and whose performance can be monitored to assure conformance to contract specifications. The contract should be awarded under competitive conditions, although this does not necessarily mean competitive bidding as such; negotiated bids seem to lead to equally satisfactory results (Edwards and Stevens, 1978).

The principal obstacle to greater competition in the delivery of public services is, not surprisingly, the opposition of employee organizations. Inevitably, therefore, the decision to proceed in this direction is a political one, not an economic one. However, as public pressure grows for greater productivity in government, the political advantages of introducing competition will become more apparent and hence more attractive to elected officials.

REFERENCES

Bish, Robert L., and Robert Warren, 1972, "Scale and Monopoly Problems in Urban Government Services," *Urban Affairs Quarterly* 8.

Bridge, Gary, 1977, "Citizen Choice in Public Services: Voucher Systems," in Savas (1977*b*).

Edwards, Franklin R., and Barbara J. Stevens, 1978, "The Provision of Municipal Sanitation Services by Private Firms: An Empirical Analysis of the Efficiency of Alternative Market Structures and Regulatory Arrangements," *Journal of Industrial Economics* 27, no. 2:133–47.

Fisk, Donald, Herbert Kiesling, and Thomas Muller, 1978, *Private Provision of Public Services: An Overview,* Washington, D.C.: Urban Institute (May).

Kirlin, John J., John C. Ries, and Sidney Sonenblum, 1977, "Alternatives to City Departments," in Savas (1977*b*).

Pacific Consultants, 1978, *Title XX: Purchase of Service,* vol. 1, Berkeley, Calif. (October).

Savas, Emanuel S., 1977, "An Empirical Study of Competition in Municipal Service Delivery," *Public Administration Review* 37, no. 6:717–24.

______, ed., 1977*a*, *The Organization and Efficiency of Solid Waste Collection,* Lexington, Mass.: Lexington Books.

______, ed., 1977*b*, *Alternatives for Delivering Public Services,* Boulder, Colo.: Westview Press.

______, 1979*a*, "Public vs. Private Refuse Collection: A Critical Review of the Evidence," *Journal of Urban Analysis* 6, no. 1.

______, 1979*b*, "How Much Does Government Service Really Cost?" *Urban Affairs Quarterly* 15, no. 1.

______, in preparation, *Private Enterprise and Public Services.*

Savas, Emanuel S., and Sigmund Ginsberg, 1973, "The Civil Service: A Meritless System?" *Public Interest* 32:70–85.

Stevens, Barbara J., 1977, "Service Arrangement and the Cost of Residential Refuse Collection," in Savas (1977*a*).

TIME, "Teaching Children at Home," December 4, 1978.

Zimmerman, Joseph F., 1973, "Meeting Service Needs through Intergovernmental Agreements," *Municipal Year Book,* Washington, D.C.: International City Management Association.

11 PUBLIC SECTOR PRODUCTIVITY AND COLLECTIVE BARGAINING: *The Case of New York City*

Eric J. Schmertz

11.1. PUBLIC SECTOR PRODUCTIVITY AND COLLECTIVE BARGAINING ISSUES

Collective bargaining on the issue of productivity appears at times to be an effort to reconcile the irreconcilable. The employer seeks to implement methods that reduce costs, increase efficiency, and raise the quantity of goods and services, while the union strives to project job security, retain work rules and benefits previously attained, insulate those with greater seniority from displacement, and gain new benefits and economic improvements (Kochan, 1980, p. 428).

In the public sector, where government at all levels has been facing increasingly severe fiscal difficulties and where the earnings of public employees have been drastically eroded by double-digit inflation, the dilemma is manifest (National Center for Productivity and Quality of Working Life, 1978, p. 54).

The problem is compounded by the fact that taxpayers have been expressing resistance to the idea of financing increased costs through higher taxes while simultaneously calling for more return on their current tax dollars. These circumstances are forcing public administrators to seek new methods for producing more and better services for each tax dollar and man-year invested. They are trying to make government more productive.

No matter how imaginative or inventive the industrial engineer, scientist, or efficiency expert may be, his new methods, work arrangements, or even mechanization may not be unilaterally adopted and implemented by an employer whose business is unionized, if, as is almost always the case, those new methods affect "wages, hours, and working conditions." Under the labor law, in both private and public sectors, an employer must "bargain" on such matters bilaterally with the union that represents his employees. Obviously, any such bargaining in which the union understandably seeks to protect the jobs and continued employment opportunities of its members, the union will, in exchange for its agreement on any new productivity methods, demand benefits that "cushion" the adverse economic impact on the employees. The "cushions" themselves may be nonproductive to the employer, thereby reducing the net productivity improvement obtained from a more efficient operation.

Thus, for an example from the private sector, there is no dispute that containerization is a much more productive, efficient, and less expensive way to load and unload cargo on ships. Yet, because its introduction by the shipping industry dramatically affected the jobs, employment rights, and tenure of unionized shipping-industry employees, the employers obtained agreement on containerization only after agreeing to union demands for improved and earlier pensions, supplemental unemployment benefits, job protection for senior employees, and savings through attrition and "gradualism." The net effect was economically beneficial to the employers and represented significant productivity improvement, but of necessity it was achieved not unilaterally and not as fully as an engineer could envision but at some price through the realistic consequences of collective bargaining (Diebold Institute, 1969).

In short, collective bargaining can and will bring about productivity improvements, but they will not be as considerable or as unlimited as if management had unconditional discretion. In my view as a labor-management practitioner, the "check and balance" of collective bargaining on the issue of productivity is a fair, equitable, and sound instrumentality in reconciling the legitimate but divergent interests of the parties involved.

Local governments have approached the goal of improving productivity from several directions—new measurement techniques, organizational changes, technological innovation, and employee motivation. However, due to the fact that government budgets are so labor intensive, that is, a large percentage of all appropriations go directly to personnel costs, opportunities for the most dramatic productivity savings are through better manpower utilization programs. While a whole range of economic and manpower factors affect government productivity, the public employee remains the key element of the entire productivity issue.

11.2. THE CASE OF THE CITY OF NEW YORK

My experience has been primarily with the City of New York and its municipal unions, particularly the unions of fire fighters and fire officers. So, I will most often refer to those collective bargaining relationships in discussing efforts to improve productivity in the public sector.

11.2.1. Issues of Practical Impact

In a case decided in 1974 by the New York City Office of Collective Bargaining (OCB), the agency created to administer the city's local collective bargaining statute, the city's right to unilaterally implement two productivity programs in the Fire Department involving reduced manning on vehicles was upheld. Although the New York City collective bargaining law calls upon both management and labor to maintain the status quo during negotiations for a new contract, the OCB (Decision No. B–13–74, p. 21) stated:

> To prohibit the City from acting during the status quo period on subjects which it could normally decide unilaterally would have the practical effect of completely immobilizing the City in its labor or personnel decisions during what is frequently a long-extended period.

The OCB added that if, as a result of the new programs instituted by the city, the fire fighters could prove a "practical impact," they would then have a right to negotiate with the city concerning ways in which the practical impact could be addressed and relieved. *Practical impact* means conditions of employment that are unduly burdensome on a continuing basis.

The practical impact concept was first dealt with by the OCB in 1968 in another case concerning fire fighters where there was a threat of a job action against the city if 2,500 additional workers were not added to the fire-fighting force. The city contended that manning is its prerogative under the management rights clause, Section 1173-4.3b of the New York City collective bargaining law (NYCCBL), which guarantees the city the power to hire and fire as well as the right to maintain efficiency and control over "the technology of performing its work." However, the section additionally provides that

> decisions of the City or any other public employer on those matters [maintaining efficiency—controlling technology of work performed] are not within the scope of collective bargaining, but, notwithstanding the above, questions concerning the *practical impact* that decisions on the above matters have on employees, such as questions of workload or manning, are within the scope of collective bargaining. [Emphasis added.]

If the OCB finds that a practical impact exists, the city is given the opportunity to act unilaterally to relieve the impact through the exercise of its reserved rights, or it may seek to relieve the impact by negotiating with the union involved over changes in wages, hours, and working conditions. If the city fails to relieve the impact in an expeditious manner or an impasse in bargaining is reached, the board will appoint an impasse panel with the authority to make recommendations to relieve the impact in question. Such recommendations can include but are not limited to calls for additional manpower or changes in work load.

Hence, though the City of New York has retained a "threshold" right to make changes in its manning of Fire Department vehicles for the purpose of improved productivity, the *effect* of any such change such as the creation of an "overwork" condition for remaining fire fighters must be dealt with and adjusted by bilateral collective bargaining.

11.2.2. Some Productivity Measurement Issues

As part of a newly structured manning plan, the city and the fire unions negotiated a method of measuring the work load of fire fighters so that a "productivity point" could be mutually determined to which fire fighters and fire units could be required to work before any claim of overwork or "practical impact" would be considered.

This "productivity" plan was titled, "Weighted Response Index" (WRI). It was much like a job evaluation system that accords points to the various activities of firemen, principally in responding to and fighting fires. The more intense and demanding fire-fighting work carries the greater point score, and a negotiated maximum point accumulation within a fixed or continuous period within a year was determined to be the point of "overwork."

It is significant to note that the original position of the unions was that work load should be measured only by the number of fire alarms to which a fire unit responded. The city pointed out that alarms differ markedly. Some are "false," involving no fire-fighting duties, and some involve multi-alarm structural fires. The WRI plan combined the differing work activities of the firemen at fires with due regard for the total quantity of alarms and types of alarms to which a unit responded. As such, the WRI represents the type of negotiated productivity plan the labor law requires, a plan that did not give all the productivity benefits to one side but that on net balance created work-load measurements and requirements that were substantially more productive or predictable than before and allowed the Fire Department to carry out its mission with less men and officers at a time of fiscal crisis.

The WRI and the attack program introduced in the Fire Department were part of an overall city policy to make operations and the delivery of services more efficient. The goal was to increase the quality and quantity of the services being performed while maintaining or cutting back on the allowed time, manpower, and costs involved.

The city soon found that public sector services that lend themselves to productivity gains that closely parallel productivity successes in the private sector are those that are easily measured—that is, garbage collection, pothole repairs, processing of papers. However, many of the activities engaged in by a municipal government that are "service oriented" rather than "product oriented" cannot be so readily measured; rather they can be judged only in terms of the quality of the service rendered, with a view to such considerations as the speed, appropriateness, and courtesy of the response offered by the city work force.

11.2.3. Productivity Bargaining in the City of New York

The city has chosen rather to bargain with the certified representatives of its employees concerning the development and adoption of such programs. One of the reasons behind this policy is the acceptance of the reality that public employees and their unions are forces to be reckoned with in governmental decision making. Perhaps equally important is the recognition of the fact that government's primary "product" is service, the delivery of which essentially depends on the employees providing those services. Therefore, while technological and managerial improvements are important, involvement of people in any change process is critical. Also, perhaps unlike the private sector, if a "productivity" change results in or is perceived by the public as a reduction in services, the bilateral agreement of the city and the affected union may be essential to obviate any union support of public opposition and to neutralize that opposition.

It is also important to realize that traditional work patterns may acquire the force of law or become institutionalized as "past practice." In that event, as a matter of law it may be necessary to negotiate with union representatives to insure that the productivity measures to be implemented meet the test of joint discussion and input. Otherwise, unlike where an employer is not unionized, the union may charge that the employer has committed the "unfair labor practice" of "refusing to bargain in good faith."

In the City of New York, productivity became an important element in the collective bargaining picture with the announcement by City Hall in December 1970 that "no salary increase is justified which is not necessary to offset inflation or is not tied to corresponding increases in worker productivity."

Two years after the announcement of the city's intention to follow a policy of exchanging wage increases for productivity gains, over 100,000 municipal workers were covered by contracts containing productivity clauses. The basic productivity language appearing in the major agreements was as follows:

> Delivery of municipal services in the most efficient, effective and courteous manner is of permanent importance to the City and the Union. Such achievement is recognized to be a mutual obligation of both parties within their respective roles and responsibilities. To achieve and maintain a high level of effectiveness the parties hereby agree to the following terms:
>
> a. The Union recognizes the City's right under the New York City Collective Bargaining Law to establish and/or revise performance standards or norms notwithstanding the existence of prior performance levels, norms or standards. Such standards, developed by usual work measurement procedures, may be used to determine acceptable performance levels, prepared work schedules and to measure the performance of each employee or group of employees. For the purpose of this Section the Union may, under Section 1173-4.3b of the New York City Collective Bargaining Law, assert to the City and/or the Board of Collective Bargaining during the term of this agreement that the City's decisions on the foregoing matters have a practical impact on employees, within the meaning of the Board of Collective Bargaining's Decision No. B-9-68. The City will give the Union prior notice of the establishment and/or revision of performance standards or norms hereunder.
> b. Employees who work at less than acceptable levels of performance may be subject to disciplinary measures in accordance with applicable law.

Examples of the types of programs introduced through productivity bargaining in the early 1970s include the following:

1. An "adaptive response" procedure in the Fire Department was introduced whereby less equipment and manpower are initially dispatched to answer an alarm with reliance on improved radio communication with which more equipment can be summoned if the conditions at the scene of a fire warrant it;
2. Changes in police scheduling permitting the city to assign more officers to the 4:00 PM to midnight shift—the high crime period—and the establishment of one-man patrol cars were introduced;
3. The elimination of caseload limits for social workers was achieved in part by reassigning paper work to clerical employees whose average salaries were $3,500 less than those of case workers;
4. Scheduling changes for the Sanitation Department were introduced allowing for the assignment of more men on Mondays, a traditionally hard day because of the garbage that normally piles up over a weekend; additionally, vacations were spread out over the year rather than being concentrated in the summer when more men are needed.
5. Resurfacing of streets and highways at night instead of during the day when such activity snarls traffic and interrupts commerce was accomplished through the payment of a 10 percent night differential.

The unique feature of these and other productivity bargaining programs implemented by the City of New York was the fact that cost-of-living adjustments were contractually linked to the savings generated by these programs.

11.2.4. Pressures for Productivity Bargaining under Fiscal Crisis

When the fiscal crisis came to a head in 1975, the city administration had to make room on the management side of the bargaining table for both the federal and state governments, the latter embodied by the Emergency Financial Control Board (EFCB). Shortly thereafter, productivity bargaining in New York City became a multilevel affair.

As part of the New York City Seasonal Financing Act, which permitted the city to borrow money from the federal treasury to alleviate its cash-flow problems, the federal government required the city to submit a revised three-year financial plan, reviewed and approved by the EFCB. The EFCB was established by New York State as part of the Financial Emergency Act for the City of New York. This 1975 law provided generally for state supervision and review of all aspects of the city's financial arrangements and specifically required EFCB approval of all labor contracts.

The Ford administration insisted that the city's financial plan include an agreement in principle with the major municipal unions that for the next contract term there be no net increases in the costs to the city of compensating its employees. Within two weeks the city and most of the municipal labor unions signed a Memorandum of Interim Understanding, also known as the Hilton Agreement, covering labor relations in the city for the period 1976–1978. The agreement was immediately brought before and approved by the EFCB, which established the following guidelines for municipal labor contracts:

1. No agreement shall provide for general wage or salary increases or increases in fringe benefits.
2. No agreement shall provide for increases or adjustments to salaries or wages, including those based upon increases in the cost of living, unless such increases or adjustments are funded by independently measured savings realized, without reduction in services, through gains in productivity, reductions of fringe benefits or through other savings or other revenues approved by the EFCB, all of which savings shall be in addition to those provided for in the financial plan.
3. Each agreement shall provide for a mechanism to permit savings in pension costs or other fringe benefits during the term of agreement.

The Hilton Agreement abided by these guidelines and provided that in return for realized productivity savings, city employees would be paid a cost-of-living adjustment (COLA) of $21 per year for each 0.4 percent increase in the city's consumer price index above the March 1976 level. In addition, both parties agreed to cut labor costs by $24 million through fringe benefit reductions or productivity savings. COLA payments were to be funded only from savings realized beyond the $24 million target figure. Layoffs of city workers were to be avoided if at all possible.

The terms of the Financial Emergency Act also covered the labor relations policies of independent municipal agencies such as the Transit Authority, the Board of Education, the Board of Higher Education, and the Housing Authority. In fact, the contract between the Transit Workers' Union and the Transit Authority was the first negotiated settlement submitted to and approved by the EFCB.

The EFCB wanted to promulgate special guidelines for the transit situation, for unlike other city workers, transit employees' COLA increases had to be funded solely from productivity savings, without the aid of "other savings" or "other revenue." In addition, the EFCB demanded that the

Transit Authority determine prior to the beginning of every month whether or not there were sufficient productivity savings to meet expected COLA payments.

Recognizing the bilateral nature of productivity as an issue in the unionized public sector and following strenuous protests from the transit unions, the EFCB relented on those aforesaid special productivity conditions and made the productivity rule for cost-of-living increases applicable to city employees generally also applicable to transit employees.

The contract between the United Federation of Teachers (UFT) and the Board of Education also underwent a lengthy approval process by the EFCB. Eventually it was agreed that COLA payments would be paid in accordance with the terms of the Hilton Agreement. It was also agreed that a panel consisting of representatives of the Board of Education, the UFT and the city would be created to develop productivity programs and determine the value of the increased productivity achieved through those programs.

When the productivity programs were developed, they were submitted to the special deputy comptroller for the City of New York for review. Specifically, his function was to confirm that the identified savings had been or could be realized and that the programs had not and would not cause a reduction in services.

It was the hope of management and labor that productivity savings would account for the bulk of monies needed for COLA payments. The city's experience with the first COLA period—October 1, 1976, through March 31, 1977—proved otherwise. Of the $6.86 million that the special comptroller found attainable from the programs submitted by the city for members of District Council 37, American Federation of State, County, and Municipal Employees, only $63,000 was attributable to productivity savings. Revenue programs would account for $5.25 million and other savings programs an even $1 million. Broken down even further, he found that of the $5.25 million attainable through revenue programs, $3.8 million was a one-time windfall made possible because of a change in state reimbursement regulations associated with welfare payments. In fact, of the programs submitted for review, approximately 65 percent of the savings were one-time affairs rather than recurring revenues or savings. Thus he and others claimed that it was evident that productivity bargaining was more successful in generating short-term rather than long-range savings.

Any discussion of productivity as a bargaining issue engenders certain skepticism and concern about the invasion of management rights and, more importantly, whether it really is possible to have effective productivity bargaining in the public sector, at least by private sector manufacturing standards. However, with at least 37 percent of the cost-of-living adjustments paid to New York City workers over the last two years funded by productivity savings, does this not demonstrate that public management and unions have made a start in promoting and can cooperate to promote the more effective delivery of public services? Most significantly, there has been the recognition by the public sector unions that they must share responsibility with public management for fiscal survival in times of bona fide fiscal crises. Contrary to the traditional private sector trade union reluctance "to be the junior partner in success and the senior partner in failure," New York City public sector unions became heavily involved in dealing with the fiscal difficulties. Albert Shanker, president of the teachers' union declared, "If the City doesn't survive, our contract isn't going to be worth a damn." He added, "If a boat is going down, you'd better get together and bail."

Victor Gotbaum, head of New York City's largest union, said, "More than 16% of our gross national product goes into the cost of local government, and the delivery of those services is often inefficient and cumbersome."

There followed, during the administration of Mayor Beame, agreement to defer wage increases and the abandonment of or reduction in such nonproductive benefits as summer hours, blood days, personal leave days, and other time away from direct rendition of services, actions that culminated in the dramatic decision of the municipal unions to invest millions of dollars of their pension fund money in city bonds, thereby contributing substantially to the city's desperate and successful effort to avert bankruptcy. Clearly, the willingness of the unions to defer wage increases, to agree to some "give-backs," to cooperate with plans for massive layoffs, to leave jobs vacant following attrition, and to make a direct financial contribution by buying city bonds, are "productivity" improvements in a financial sense at a time when money had to be saved, if not traditional "productivity" improvements in an engineering sense. The fact is that the end result, a less costly operation of municipal services, was achieved through bilateral negotiations on the general issue of productivity.

However, the program's detractors have claimed that productivity-funded COLA payments were essentially a failure. They point to the same aforesaid statistic, namely that just 37 percent of the $81 million in COLA payments made to municipal employees over the prior years was the result of savings generated by employee productivity gains or reduced fringe benefits. The majority of the funds came from cutbacks in the size of the city's work force, management initiatives, or other city revenues.

A report expressing this view went on to say that there is significant potential for supplying municipal services at a lower cost and improving the quality of the services provided as well. Productivity is still a viable technique for improving the city's financial picture and it is up to the city, the report concludes, to monitor employee work practices and output more closely.

Under the administration of Mayor Koch, the Coalition Economic Agreement signed on June 20, 1978, covering most of the city's employees, does not contain any provision for productivity-funded COLAs but does provide that unpaid COLAs from the prior contract period be paid in a lump sum without regard to the availability of productivity savings to fund such payments. However on January 26, 1979, Mayor Koch, by executive order, established the Productivity Council. The stated purpose of the council is to develop and seek to implement methods for enhancing the productivity of the city's labor force. Under this new arrangement, it is hoped that strides will be made to bring the following remarks by the special deputy comptroller to fruition: "A commitment to learn from the mistakes of the past, to exercise available management controls and to achieve closer cooperation from labor could make this second attempt more successful than the first" (Report of the Office of the Special Deputy Comptroller for New York City, December 1978, p. ii).

11.3. CONCLUSION

Reviewing the history of productivity bargaining in the City of New York over the past decade, it is clear that productivity is not, as some early commentators claimed, the latest in a long series of management fads or techniques that would be short-lived and soon forgotten. Rather it is a concept—the relationship of what we are getting for what we are investing—that is of enduring importance to all governmental bodies at every level.

If productivity improvements are achieved in any city's services, the success is often chiefly attributable to city hall support, managerial leadership, and union cooperation—in short, through collective bargaining.

Management should be sensitive to the need for educating its employees about proposed productivity changes. Union opposition can be minimized by dealing with union leaders as stakeholders in the city's future. Reliance on traditional management tools to improve the effectiveness and efficiency of conventional public service operations has proven to be well placed. Possibly, what is needed now is the development of new approaches to meeting public goals, or in redefining public goals as a means of improving resource utilization. With the creation of the new Productivity Council, the

City of New York now has a mechanism for improving communication with an emphasis on the common purpose and common objectives of both management and labor and a forum for discussion that is at least partially free from the pressure and point-making atmosphere of the bargaining table.

The pursuit of productivity improvements in the City of New York has established the principle that although civil servants are entitled to wages and benefits comparable to those of their counterparts in the private sector, the tax-paying public is equally entitled to comparable efficiency and quality of work. Beyond the desirability of achieving higher quality and effectiveness in the essential services that government provides, the importance of improving productivity goes directly to the need for maintaining public confidence in government and faith in the competence of public services.

REFERENCES

Diebold Institute for Public Policy Studies, 1969, *Labor-Management Contracts and Technological Change,* New York: Praeger.

Kochan, Thomas A., 1980, *Collective Bargaining and Industrial Relations,* Homewood, Ill.: Richard D. Irwin.

National Center for Productivity and Quality of Working Life, 1978, *Productivity in the Changing World of the 1980's: The Final Report of the National Center for Productivity and Quality of Working Life,* Washington, D.C.: Gov't. Printing Office.

NAME INDEX

SUBJECT INDEX